OSKAR LAMBERT KÜRTEN PhD was born in Anleur, Belgium, in 1886. He lost his hearing during his student years, becoming almost completely deaf. Despite this, he held a senior position in the Berlin State Statistical Office for over 50 years. Kürten developed an interest in spiritual world-views and had an inner experience that anthroposophy was his personal path. He lived for and out of anthroposophy, especially Rudolf Steiner's Christ impulse, publishing three books on the theme. He died in Berlin in 1973.

I0799466

SYMPHONIES OF CREATION

The Primal Elementary Kingdoms in the Work of Rudolf Steiner

Oskar Kürten

Translated by Paul King

TEMPLE LODGE

Temple Lodge Publishing Ltd.
Hillside House, The Square
Forest Row, RH18 5ES

www.templelodge.com

Published in English by Temple Lodge 2018

Originally published in German under the title *Über die Elementarreiche in der Darstellung Rudolf Steiners: Studienmaterial zur anthroposophisch orientierten Geisteswissenschaft* by Verlag Die Pforte, Basel 1990

A CIP catalogue record for this book is available from the British Library

ISBN 978 1 912230 20 4

Cover by Morgan Creative featuring image © Styleuneed
Typeset by DP Photosetting, Neath, West Glamorgan
Printed and bound by 4Edge Ltd., Essex

Contents

Introduction by Paul King 1

I. The Elementary Kingdoms

1. The elementary kingdoms as time periods and as realms of beings 3
2. The Three Worlds and the Spirit World in particular 11
   - 2.1 • The Three Worlds 11
   - 2.2 • The World of Spirits 14
3. The elementary kingdoms as form-creating thought-seed beings and as the shaping forces of the kingdoms of nature 25
4. The entrance of the elementary kingdoms into earth evolution and how they appear to clairvoyant vision 36
5. The elementary kingdoms' formative forces as divine sacrifice 45
6. The elementary kingdoms as the life kernels of the kingdoms of nature 55
   - 6.1 • Life Kernels 58
   - 6.2 • The life kernels' unfolding of being through group egos 61
   - 6.3 • Working-together of elementary kingdoms and the group egos 65
   - 6.4 • The elementary kingdoms and the states of matter 67
7. Substances in the subtle 'garments' of the life kernel 75
   - 7.1 • The primordial substance and its forms of densification 75
   - 7.2 • Substances as living beings 81
8. The elementary kingdoms and the beings of the elemental world 89
9. Influence of the elementary kingdoms on sleeping human beings 97
10. The elementary kingdoms as hidden predisposition in the human members-of-being 108
    - 10.1 • The relation of the elementary kingdoms to the lower human members-of-being and to the third hierarchy 111
    - 10.2 • The future development of the higher members-of-being 119

11. The Shaping of the Human Members-of-Being by the Elementary Kingdoms 127
11.1 • The Creation of the lower members-of-being 127
11.2 • Laying down the rudiments of the higher members of the human being 129
12. The passage of the earth through the elementary kingdoms and the Stages of Form 135

II. The Elemental World

1. The elemental world as the world of etheric forces 147
2. Attributes of the elemental world 154
3. The structuring of the ethers in the earth's physical Stage of Form 159

III. The Spiritual Organism of the earth—Planetary Spirit (a fragment) 165

Appendix
Overview of Stages of Evolution 169
Regions of the Spirit World 170

Bibliography 171

Further Reading 176

Introduction

In many quarters today the human being is regarded as nothing more than a complex biological machine, having evolved through a random series of natural selections with no meaning. With the development of artificial intelligence and impending artificial super-intelligence that is threatening to explode into our lives, there are enthusiastic plans to 'improve' and mechanize the human being with AI implants, virtual reality receivers and other extreme technologies. In the face of all this, the real nature and grandeur of the human as a spiritual being is in grave peril of being entirely lost. Counterbalancing this trend is a picture of the stupendous spiritual complexities and harmonies that lie behind the evolution of humanity (and all the beings involved with the earth), a 'mental sword', if you will, to help neutralize as far as possible the negative effects of the 'anti-human' aspects of AI and transhumanism. Such a picture, I believe, is presented in this publication.

When I first discovered this book in German, I asked a number of German speakers interested in anthroposophy if they had heard of Oskar Kürten. The strange thing is, none of them had. I say strange, because when I read the book I was astounded at what Kürten had achieved in it.

Symphonies of Creation is the life's work* of a man who, due to severe deafness, led a retiring life, and fulfilled his outer work at the Berlin State Statistical Office. His inner work, however, was of a completely different nature, the results of which are before you.

The 'elementary kingdoms' of the subtitle are not to be confused with the elemental realms of the beings behind the classical elements we know as Fire, Air, Water, and Earth. The elementary kingdoms of this book are aspects of the lofty spiritual realms from which *all* creation has arisen. They are the realms of formative forces that provide successive life-waves of being with their subtle and bodily 'garments' as vehicles through which evolution becomes possible. Behind the physical and subtle bodies of minerals, plants, animals, and humanity, are realms of creativity. Beginning as undefined 'intention' in the mind of divine-spiritual beings, Everything-That-Is-To-Be then passes to slightly lower levels where

* Oskar Kürten also published three booklets on Christological themes:
— *Der Sonnengeist Christus in der Darstellung von Rudolf Steiner* (The Sun Spirit of Christ in the work of Rudolf Steiner)
— *Der Sohnesgott, der Logos und die Trinität* (The Son God, the Logos, and the Trinity)
— *Jesus von Nazareth* (Jesus of Nazareth)

'intention' begins to 'crystallize' as thought-form archetypes. Continuing the descent, the archetypes gradually individualize and are clothed in astrality, ethericity, and finally the physical minerality of what we see with our senses. This vast process is the harmonious work of countless spiritual beings. The formative energies behind it all, however, are the forces of the elementary kingdoms. 'No true understanding of the world,' Kürten writes, 'is possible without an understanding of the elementary kingdoms.'

Steiner spoke on many occasions and in different places of these kingdoms and the multiple processes involved in them. Kürten has sought out these references (his bibliography covers some 85 GA numbers), inwardly meditated and digested them, and presented them in an inwardly cohesive form. Even for individuals who have been studying anthroposophy for decades, this can present startling new insights.

Kürten's style is matter-of-fact and self-effacing. Mostly he lets the quotes speak for themselves, himself introducing and placing them in such a way as to clarify and deepen the subject. His enumeration of lists of beings and stages of evolution may seem dry at times, even 'mathematical'. And indeed from a certain perspective the subject *is* mathematical, but in the sense that music is mathematical. Kürten presents us with the 'musical score' of the great cosmic symphony in which every section of the orchestra has its part to play and its unique qualities and motifs to contribute. By itself, the score of a Beethoven symphony is also dry and mathematical. What it represents, however, is something magnificent. So Kürten also gives us something magnificent, something about as far from 'meaningless natural selection' as is conceivably possible—the reality behind the 'score'—the Symphony of Creation.

Paul King
July 2018

Translator's note:
The author's interpolations in quoted text are shown in square brackets [like this].
The translator's interpolations in any part of the text are shown in curly brackets {like this}.

I. THE ELEMENTARY KINGDOMS

1. The elementary kingdoms as time periods and as realms of beings

Just as the word 'element' signifies fundamental substance, basic component, so the 'elementary kingdoms' as described by Rudolf Steiner are conditions of existence which preceded, and are the origin of, present earth existence, and are still the active forces behind it. This gives a double meaning to the idea of elementary kingdoms: namely, as a *developmental phase* in time, and as a *realm of beings* at a particular stage of development. When elementary kingdoms are referred to in spiritual scientific discourse it is therefore important to be aware of the sense in which they are to be understood.

The cycle of creation to which our solar system and earth belong, evolves through seven *planetary* conditions of existence which serve to develop the different stages of consciousness of its beings. Of these seven planetary stages, three have already passed—the Saturn, Sun and Moon existences. The present earth development is the fourth planetary stage; and this will be followed in the future by evolutions in the Jupiter, Venus and Vulcan stages.

Each of these evolutionary planetary stages is divided into seven great sub-divisions referred to as *Life Stages*, *realms*, *great cycles* or *Rounds*. And it is the first three of these periods, these Life Stages or Rounds, that in spiritual science are regarded as the *elementary kingdoms*. The four subsequent periods are the 'mineral kingdom', the 'plant kingdom', the 'animal kingdom', and the 'human kingdom'. Our earth development has already passed through the three elementary kingdoms, and is now in the fourth kingdom, the mineral kingdom. 'Mineral kingdom' here, in the esoteric sense, does not signify directly what is usually understood by this term—crystalline and other mineral structures—but a particular period within planetary development. The same applies to the plant, animal and human kingdoms. These elemental and other kingdoms as successive periods will be explored in Chapter 12.

But 'elementary kingdom' can also refer to the *beings* at one of the Life-Stage levels designated as elementary kingdoms. For all beings evolve through the seven Life Stages or kingdoms, so that within every planetary evolution there are beings undergoing development in each of these seven kingdoms. The beings at the first Life Stage comprise the first elementary kingdom; those at the second stage comprise the second; and those at the third Life Stage, the third elementary kingdom. Likewise during every planetary evolution there are beings belonging to the mineral, plant, animal and human kingdoms. The beings at these higher Life Stages are not strictly elementary kingdoms any longer, but they are nevertheless sometimes referred to as such by Rudolf Steiner.

Thus already during the Saturn, Sun and Moon periods there were beings belonging to each of the three elementary kingdoms, and there are likewise such beings in our present earth existence. A mineral, plant, animal, and human kingdom also existed on the previous embodiments of the earth; however, these kingdoms on Saturn, Sun and Moon were of a completely different nature from those on earth. This is why descriptions of the elementary kingdoms for earth development cannot simply be applied to earlier conditions:

> It is easier to describe them [the elementary kingdoms] for the earth, even though at the present time it is extraordinarily difficult to give people an idea of the elementary kingdoms.... Perhaps you will be able to form a picture of the three kingdoms if we say the following: So think of stones, metals and so on, and then imagine these members of the mineral kingdom becoming increasingly rarefied so that you see them less and less, so that they dissolve so to speak into more and more rarefied substantiality. Imagine they vaporize, so that they are of a totally rarefied substantiality that you can see right through, that is invisible to you.... From such structures, if we brought them to ever greater rarefaction, something would arise that in the end was no longer the mineral kingdom but the first elementary kingdom. Then we would ascend to the second and to the third elementary kingdom. It is difficult for the quality of sensitivity today to get an idea of these kingdoms which are hidden away, condensed into our world. For that is what it is like: as though these elementary kingdoms are condensed, or we could say have vanished, into our world. (GA 104, 27 June 1908)

This 'becoming increasingly rarefied' of mineral substance in the transition to the elementary kingdoms can give just a preliminary notion of these mysterious realms of being but must not be misunderstood; they are conditions of existence of such a rarefied nature that they are not accessible to perception by the senses. Indeed, they are not of a physical-mineral nature at all, but of a super-physical one; nevertheless, like the outer perceptible kingdoms of nature, they too belong to earth existence.

The beings who at present are at the mineral-kingdom level are human beings. In the Saturn phase they were at the first elemental-kingdom level, in the Sun phase at the second, and in the Moon phase in the third elementary kingdom. And just as human beings went through the elementary kingdoms before reaching the mineral kingdom, so it is also for the animals, plants and minerals. Minerals only entered evolution during the present earth existence; they are at the first Life Stage and therefore in the first elementary kingdom. The plants, which began their development as the first elementary kingdom during the Old Moon phase, are now in the second elementary kingdom. The animals lived in the first elementary kingdom on Old Sun, in the second elementary kingdom on Old Moon, and are now in the third elementary kingdom. In the usual sense, it is the minerals, appearing in physical form, which comprise the mineral kingdom of the earth; but in the esoteric sense they are only in the first elementary kingdom. The same applies for plants and animals. Only man, in this esoteric sense, is at the level of the mineral kingdom.

The beings of the third hierarchy, who stand above human beings, also passed through the elementary kingdoms during the previous embodiments of the earth. On Old Saturn the angels were in the second elementary kingdom, and the archangels in the third. The Spirits of Personality, who rose to the human level during Old Saturn by attaining ego-consciousness, belonged at that time to the fourth kingdom, the mineral kingdom, like human beings of present earth existence. These beings had undergone the first stages of their development in the elementary kingdoms of the cosmic {planetary} system that preceded our own. Since then these beings of the third hierarchy have risen to higher kingdoms. The angels now live in the plant kingdom, the archangels in the animal kingdom, and the Spirits of Personality in the human kingdom. The present earth beings will also gradually ascend to these higher kingdoms.

The human kingdom, at present at the mineral-kingdom stage, has arisen from the elementary kingdoms of the preceding embodiments of the earth.

> You will recall from *Occult Science* that the mineral kingdom did not exist during the earlier embodiments of the earth.... The mineral kingdom only arose on the earth, the fourth embodiment of the earth.... It is a difficult matter, but of extraordinary importance. There had to be three previous formations before the mineral kingdom of the earth took shape. We call these formations the three elementary

kingdoms; the mineral kingdom is the fourth. (GA 184, 8 September 1918)

That this indication cannot be referring to what is usually called the mineral kingdom of crystals and so on, follows from the fact that *this* mineral kingdom only arose on earth and did not emerge from previous formations.

At the beginning of earth evolution, in accordance with a general cosmic law, the conditions of the Old Saturn, Sun, and Moon phases were briefly recapitulated at a higher level. This occurred during the first three Life Stages of earth development. During these phases of recapitulation therefore, human beings, who are now in the mineral kingdom, had first to pass once again through the elementary kingdoms. 'The elementary kingdoms precede our mineral kingdom.... So in the early periods of earth development this mineral kingdom was present in the elementary kingdoms in an elemental state.' (GA 104, 27 June 1908)

In the present fourth Life Stage of earth evolution, we therefore find beings of the three elementary kingdoms, as well as beings of the mineral, plant, animal, and human kingdoms. When, after the three phases of recapitulation, earth development had entered the fourth Life Stage but was still in the etheric condition that preceded the present physical state, 'we need to imagine the earth, where it condensed as a subtle etheric body out of its preceding astral stage, as a conglomeration of etheric mineral mass, of etheric plant-, animal- and human beings. And also present then, as though filling in the space in between and permeating the other beings, are the creations of the three elementary kingdoms.' (GA 11, 'The Life of the Earth') Since then, minerals, plants, animals, and human beings have condensed out of the supersensory etheric state into the visible physical one; alongside them are also the beings of the three elementary kingdoms which have remained supersensory. Earth existence is composed of these seven kingdoms, and in such a way that within the earthly sphere the beings of the three elementary kingdoms comprise a world of their own, yet at the same time permeate the other earth beings, including human beings. Accordingly, the beings of the elementary kingdoms are partly active directly in human beings, animals, plants, and minerals, and partly comprise a realm of supersensory existence outside the other earthly beings, and yet belong to earth existence. It is comparatively difficult to get an accurate idea of the relation of the kingdoms of nature, including human beings, to the elementary kingdoms that lie as active forces behind them. This book is intended to serve as an aid in this.

The world of the elementary kingdoms does not only permeate and energize us human beings, but also enters into a particular relationship with us during sleep.

> When the human being sleeps, his Ego and astral body are to a certain extent in a supersensory world, but one permeating the earthly sense-world and bound up with it. So we need to make a clear distinction: there is initially a supersensory world in which human beings exist between death and a new birth; they pass through this. We can describe it as a pre-earthly or post-earthly existence.... But during sleep, the Ego and astral body are in a different supersensory world from this world of pre-earthly existence. The supersensory world of pre-earthly existence does not actually have much to do with the earth as it appears externally; whereas the supersensory world in which initially the astral body and Ego must find themselves between falling asleep and waking up has a great deal to do with the beings on earth, a great deal to do with the three kingdoms which are human beings' companions on earth. This supersensory world consists of the three so-called elementary kingdoms which you find described in my book *Theosophy*. So, apart from finding their way {between incarnations} into the world where angels and archangels are, the Ego and astral body, between falling asleep and waking up, must also live in a supersensory world which as such does not have anything directly to do with the supersensory world where angels and archangels are and in which the human being exists when not incarnated, but is a world of elementary kingdoms in which beings are to be found who are not as high as the human being when on earth, who do not have an immediate physical body, and yet are not of a purely supersensory nature. These beings of the elementary kingdoms inhabit, as it were, the other three earthly kingdoms which manifest externally. (GA 222, 12 March 1923)

It becomes clear from these short indications that the elementary kingdoms, as realms of being that are hidden within our visible world, present a difficult but very important area of study for an anthroposophically oriented Spiritual Science. Their significance is already apparent from the fact that Rudolf Steiner devoted in his foundational book *Theosophy* (GA 9) a detailed section to these elementary kingdoms, 'The Physical World and its Connection with the Soul and Spirit Lands'. Also in his lectures he indicates on many occasions how important knowledge of the elementary kingdoms is for an understanding of the world. For, as will be seen, they are at work invisibly as *shape-creating formative forces of cosmic thought* in everything that manifests sense-perceptibly or supersensibly in all the forms of the kingdoms of nature and in man. The formless physical-mineral element {for example water and gases}, and mineral crystals; the diversity of physical structures in the plant with its roots, leaves, flowers and fruits; the multiform, sometimes beautiful, sometimes bizarre physical appearances of the animal kingdom; and the forms of people, not one of which is the same as the other—all these are constructed by the elementary kingdoms using the forces of cosmic thought. The same applies to etheric bodies (the bearers of life), and to the astral bodies that bring about sensation and consciousness in animals and man. Even the human individual's Ego-structure (*Ich-Glied*), the bearer of human thought life, is formed by an elementary kingdom. The creative, shape-giving activity of the elementary kingdoms is thus the basis of all phenomena through which 'being' comes into manifestation. In view of the relatively few indications given by Rudolf Steiner concerning the elementary kingdoms, we can only attempt in the following to investigate some of the hidden connections existing between these mysterious forces and earthly creations. It is important not to confuse elementary kingdoms with elemental *beings* who are at work as forces of nature, even though there is a close connection between these two kinds of being, as their similar name suggests.

We must therefore distinguish between *being a kingdom* in the usual sense, and *being incarnated in a kingdom* in the occult sense. As beings of a particular kind, minerals, plants, animals, and human beings each comprise a kingdom of their own. Among these earthly creatures only the human being is incarnated in the strict sense. Human beings awaken in their physical-mineral body to self-awareness. By perceiving a world outside themselves—to which their own body belongs—and by distinguishing themselves from it, human beings experiences themselves as an Ego being. As an Ego we attain consciousness of ourselves and can also have cognition of the surrounding physical-mineral world. Thus the mineral kingdom is for human beings the foundation of their physical existence; they are incarnated in the mineral kingdom.

> The lay person would say today's minerals belong to the mineral kingdom, the plants to the plant kingdom. From the lay perspective this is correct, but in an occult sense it is incorrect. For, today only human beings are completely in the mineral kingdom. They will ascend in future periods of evolution to the plant, animal, and human kingdoms. Because we have an Ego-consciousness, we can definitely call present-day humans 'human,' but we cannot say, from an occult scientific point of view, that they are incarnated in the human king-

dom.... This human being, which we ourselves are, is basically the only being that has developed fully in the mineral kingdom, while the other kingdoms in many respects are at a much lower level than what is designated as the mineral kingdom in occultism. (GA 104, 27 June 1908)

During earth existence, through our sense organs and the intellect bound to the physical brain, we can understand and master only the mineral kingdom. We need only think of how human beings use technology to exploit mineral forces in a growing range of applications, produce new synthetic substances, alter and split matter unleashing enormous sources of energy. Only when human beings have learnt to understand and manipulate plant life in the same way as we manipulate things today in the dead mineral kingdom, will we be incarnated in the plant kingdom. We will reach this level at the Jupiter stage. At the Venus stage human beings will understand and master the nature of animal sentience, and thereby be incarnated in the animal kingdom. Finally, in Vulcan, we will fully understand the nature of the human *being* and only then will we be incarnated in the human kingdom.

What can human beings comprehend today? That is the point. Today they can only understand the mineral kingdom. As soon as they come to the plant, they no longer understand it. But the mineral kingdom they can understand, they can construct machines, houses and so on from mineral forces. When in the same way they learn to fathom the forces in a plant that make it grow, only then will their consciousness rise into the plant kingdom. And when they learn to comprehend how an animal can have sensations and feelings—at present we can only have an external view of this—that will make them a member of the animal kingdom. And when individuals do not only grasp their own 'I', but another 'I', when they inwardly comprehend another human being completely, only then will they belong to the human kingdom. (GA 104, 27 June 1908)

In the mineral kingdom, human beings learn to feel themselves as an independent, individual personality. In the future, as they rise into higher kingdoms, they will feel themselves more and more as belonging to the whole of humanity.

When human beings reach the level of the plant kingdom, their whole life will be different. They will not feel themselves as a personality, but, just as today they do feel themselves as a personality, they will feel themselves as a human being, they will feel themselves as a part of all humanity. When, for example, they have reached the plant kingdom, they will find it unbearable that they have a certain amount of happiness when near them there is someone who is unhappy. . . . And at an even higher stage the individual human being will be part of the whole, when they are at the sixth stage; and then even more in the seventh stage, when they are human in the fullest sense, a completely spiritualized human being. (GA 184, 8 September 1918)

2. The Three Worlds and the Spirit World in particular

2.1 The Three Worlds

The elementary kingdoms operate in the three worlds in which the development of the earth's beings takes place. Thus, to understand the elementary kingdoms, a knowledge of the structure of these worlds is first required. The three worlds are the spiritual, astral (soul) and physical worlds. The spiritual world is the primordial world sufficient unto itself; the other two emerge from it by a process of densification, as it were, and dissolve back into it again. The astral world thus reveals itself as spirit in soul form, and the physical world as spirit condensed to the point of material manifestation.

As mentioned earlier, the evolution of our creation cycle goes through seven planetary conditions or Stages of Consciousness. In each of these planetary developments it passes through seven Life Stages (kingdoms, great cycles or Rounds). Each Life Stage is divided in turn into seven sub-divisions, called Stages of Form, lesser cycles or Globes. Consciousness, Life and Form are the creative forces at the basis of all evolution.

The Stages of Form are conditions of existence of different kinds, beginning at the highest, purely spiritual condition, descending through increasing degrees of density to the point of physical materialization, and then ascending again to spiritualization at the original level of departure. This gives us the following seven Stages of Form:

1. the arupa plane or higher spirit world (upper Devachan)
2. the rupa plane or lower spirit world (lower Devachan)
3. the astral plane or soul world
4. the physical plane
5. the astral plane
6. the rupa plane
7. the arupa plane.

The development of each Life Stage is thus accomplished by passing through seven Stages of Form. The two form stages at the top, the arupa and rupa planes, are the spiritual world in the strictest sense, the land of spirits. Spiritual science also speaks of an elemental and an etheric world; these however are not specific worlds in themselves but transitional stages from the astral to the physical world. We will look at them in more detail later on.

At present the earth is in the fourth Life Stage, and in the fourth—the physical—Stage of Form, to which it has evolved by descent from the arupa plane through the rupa and astral planes. This physical Stage of Form is the densest; from here evolution ascends again to spiritual existence on the arupa plane. The Stages of Form that arise during the descent from the arupa plane to physical denseness, remain; they only dissolve again in sequence with the re-ascent to arupa. Accordingly at the beginning and end of each Life Stage there is only one Stage of Form present, the arupa condition. In the middle of each Life Stage by contrast, at the fourth Stage of Form, there are four different conditions of form that overlap, for these conditions are not separate from one another but interpenetrate. (GA 104, 27 June 1908, not quoted)

In the process of re-spiritualizing from the physical condition to arupa, the beings are enriched by what they have experienced and undergone during their descent through the Form Stages. Because of this, the Stages of Form during the evolutionary re-ascent are not the same as those during descent. Rather, the ascending Stages of Form represent a higher level of development, so we need to speak here not of passage through just four stages, but indeed through seven different form conditions. Each passage through the seven Stages of Form means a higher level of development for the beings, an increase of forces and capacities with which they then move to the next Life Stage.

In this descent and re-ascent through the conditions of Form the *law of cyclical development* is evident. For development does not consist of a process always moving forward: at a certain point it begins to retrace its path, but at a higher level. All evolution is followed by involution. It is like a circular, spiral movement back to the point of origin but at a higher level. 'The basic character of the world is that which is cyclical and circular.' (GA 138, 29 August 1912)

Each Stage of Consciousness, Life, and Form is separated from the others by a kind of outward condition of rest. It is an intermediate state in which everything dissolves, as it were; all externality turns inwards and is only present in seed form. This condition, called *pralaya*, nevertheless signifies lively activity in higher spiritual worlds in which the seeds are prepared for a new development in manifest form. 'All the beings and forces have returned to spirit again. During this process of spiritualization they have ascended to higher worlds. The lowest of the worlds in which anything can still be observed during this spiritualized phase is the same one in which the human being of the present bides between death and a new birth. They are regions of spirit land.' (GA 13 *Die Weltenentwickelung und der Mensch*, Abschnitt über die Erdenentwickelung (*World Evolution and Man*, section on the evolution of the earth))

At the end of this cosmic night, as it were, everything that is going to develop appears initially in the consciousness of higher divine-spiritual beings on the arupa plane for a new passage through the three worlds. In the meantime the fruits of the previous evolution have been wrought into new thought-seeds from which a new world can arise. For, every world-creation is founded on the experience of a previous evolution whose fruits are preserved as seed thoughts in the memory of divine creative powers. This is 'creation out of nothing,' that is, out of thoughts gained by experience. (GA 93a, 30 October 1905, not quoted)

Such a passage through the Stages of Life and Form is like a monumental rhythm of breath—the highest worlds of gods breathe out the beings, as it were, to gain experience in the three worlds, then breathe them in once more, whereupon the same process is repeated at a higher level.

Each Stage of Form also goes through seven sub-divisions, called 'Principal Ages' or 'epochs' by Rudolf Steiner. Theosophical literature calls them root races or principal races. These Principal Ages are:

1. the Polarean epoch
2. the Hyperborean epoch
3. the Lemurian epoch
4. the Atlantean epoch
5. the post-Atlantean epoch
6. —
7. —

In our epoch, four of these Principal Ages have already passed; we live in the fifth, the post-Atlantean epoch.

Each Principal Age is again divided into seven eras, which in our post-Atlantean development are called Cultural Periods. These Cultural Periods are:

1. the ancient Indian period
2. the ancient Persian period
3. the Chaldean-Egyptian period
4. the Greco-Roman period
5. the Middle European period
6. —
7. —

Thus in the cosmic plan all sequences of time are ordered according to the number seven.

2.2 The World of Spirits

The spirit world, in the true and strictest sense, encompasses the two higher Stages of Form, the arupa and rupa planes. It is divided into seven sections or regions, of which the arupa plane forms the three higher regions, and the rupa plane the four lower. The spirit world is a world of living thought-beings. All the beings of this world consist of pure thought, of which human thought is but a pale and shadowy image. 'With the strengthened soul, one lives there into a world which reveals itself in such a way that beings are present in it that consist of thought-substance, but in a way that is more alive, more personal, more individual and far more real than human beings on earth.' (GA 147, 29 August 1913)

In the spirit world, thoughts are living creative beings whose 'words are deeds', that is, cause forms and structures to arise. The thought-substance of which these beings of the spirit world consist, contains the forces that give what manifests in the astral and physical world its form. This thought-substance is the bearer of the divine thought that is the foundation of the world, the substance into which the gods implant their intentions and goals for the formation of the world. The spirit world thus reveals itself as a world of *formative thought-forces* creating structures and form.

The arupa world, also called the World of Reason (*Vernunftwelt*), is the world of Intuition. The actual Akashic Chronicle is also found here, which preserves the spiritual counter-images of everything that happens in the three worlds. Imprints, quasi reflections of this Akashic Chronicle can also be perceived in the rupa and astral worlds. The rupa world, also called the mental or heavenly world, is the world of Inspiration, the world of the harmony of the spheres; it reveals itself as a sounding world. Arupa means 'formless', the potential for form; rupa means 'formed'. In the arupa world the thoughts are still spirit-seeds without form; here they are not yet shaped into concrete thought-images but lie, as yet undeveloped, as intentions, impulses, goals in the consciousness of the higher hierarchies. This is the world of *still-formless thought seed beings*. Rudolf Steiner also calls them 'living seed points'. We can regard the arupa condition as a seed state in which everything that is to unfold is still at rest in a germinal condition—a germinal state full of creative forces for impending development.

Only on the rupa plane do the thought seeds of arupa take shape as specific thought forms, as thought archetypes. The rupa world is the world of formed thoughts, the *world of archetypes* or the *realm of forms*. The thought archetypes arising here are like spiritual models according to which the shapes and forms in the soul and physical worlds emerge.

Thought archetypes are the ideas that come to expression in manifest phenomena, and are reflected in human consciousness as thoughts.

Steiner writes about this rupa world of archetypes in his *Theosophy*:

> Now in this world can be seen the spiritual archetypes of all things that exist in the physical and soul worlds. . . . Such archetypes for everything are contained in the actual 'World of Spirit', and physical things and beings are images or imitations of these archetypes. . . . In their true form the archetypes are very dissimilar from their sense-perceptible images. And just as dissimilar are their shadows—abstract thoughts.
>
> In the spiritual world everything is in constant movement and activity, in unceasing creativity. . . . For the archetypes are *creative beings*. They are the master crafters of everything that arises in the physical and soul worlds. They change shape quickly; and in each archetype there is the potential to take on countless different forms. They cause a particular shape to sprout up, as it were, out of themselves, and no sooner is this generated than the archetype sets about bubbling up the next one.
>
> And archetypes are to varying degrees connected and related to each other. They do not act in isolation. Each needs the help of the other for its creating. Often countless archetypes work together so that this or that structure can arise in the soul or physical world.' (GA 9, *The Three Worlds III*)

Thus, for example, an immense number of archetypes need to unite and work together to bring about the infinitely complex human physical body with its limbs and many organs, and establish a harmonious collaboration between them.

The seed thoughts for the archetypes in the lower regions of spirit land belong to the three higher regions. For the beings here give the archetypes of the lower regions the *impulses* for their activity. We find in them the creative forces of the archetypes themselves. Anyone able to ascend to these regions becomes acquainted with the 'intentions' that are behind our world. The archetypes lie here like living germinal points, ready to take up the most diverse forms from the thought-entities. Once these germinal points have been guided to the lower regions, they swell up as it were, and manifest themselves in the most diverse forms. (GA 9, *The Three Worlds III*) It is these spiritual formations that the human mind perceives—albeit as shadowy reflections—when it tries to reach an understanding of sense-perceptible things through thinking.

Thus everything that manifests in astral form in the soul world, and in physical form in the sense world, is founded on an 'intention' in the higher, and a 'thought archetype' in the lower spirit regions. The archetype creates a condensed image of itself, as it were, from the substances of the lower worlds. And when human beings create mental pictures and thoughts about sense-perceptible phenomena, then the archetypes themselves are reflected in a mysterious way as shadowy images in their thinking. Without being aware of it, human beings experience in their thoughts about the things of the senses the living thought-forms of the archetypes, albeit not in their true stature, but as abstract thoughts.

> The life of human thought belongs in truth to the spiritual world; but the way it emerges in physical existence is such that its true form is veiled. We can say that the thought life of the physical human being is a shadow image, an imitation of the true spiritual being to which it belongs. (GA 9, *The Three Worlds IV*)

> Only because the things of the sense-perceptible world are none other than condensed spirit-beings is it possible for the human being, who lifts himself up to these spirit-beings in thought, to understand things in his thinking. The things of the senses originate in the spiritual world, ... and when someone thinks about these things, then his attention (*Inneres*) is simply directed away from the sense-perceptible form of the things and to their spiritual archetypes. (GA 9, *The Three Worlds V*)

Everything thought by gods in the past, and out of which the present world with its earthly kingdoms of nature arose and continues to exist, is contained in the seed thoughts of the arupa world. They are the gods' memory images, so to speak, from past cosmic ages, which have been preserved as seeds from which the mineral, plant, and animal kingdoms of nature develop. Divine thoughts that are alive *in the present* are at work only in human beings. Thoughts are poured into the thought-seed substance of the arupa world and then, in the world of archetypes, the soul world, and in the sense world, are realized, creating and shaping, in the human kingdom.

Thus the operation of the divine-spiritual hierarchies in *nature* on the earth is not of the immediate present. Outer nature that surrounds us is work left behind by previous divine-spiritual activity.

> This work, in its forms, is of a divine-spiritual kind through and through. For human perception the divine is evident in the forms, in natural events, but it is no longer a living element there. Nature is this god-enacted work of the divine and is everywhere an image of divine activity. (GA 26, letter of 25 October 1924)

> To look into this world with understanding means to have forms and shapes before one which speak eloquently of the divine, but in which self-living divine existence cannot be found, if one does not delude oneself. (GA 26, letter of 2 November 1924)

> This is how it is in nature in the mineral, plant, and animal kingdoms. In these kingdoms live the thoughts of divine-spiritual beings that were thought in the past; and they continue in the living existence of the present much like our memories in our soul life. Thus we do not have in the world around us the thoughts of divine-spiritual beings as they are living directly in the present, but the gods' memories, the preserved thoughts of the gods. (GA 141, 11 February 1913)

> In the whole of nature, when the human being is removed from it, there are no gods. . . . This entire world, disregarding human beings, is something that the gods have separated off out of themselves in the course of evolution. . . . What we have as the world around us is something of the past. When we look out at nature we see the spirit's past, something left behind from this spiritual past. . . . For we should not imagine that there is anything present in this outer world that is the actual divine-spiritual being that creates human beings. Certainly there are elemental beings, lower spiritual beings. . . . Among what remains from this divine past there are elemental beings and so on. (GA 198, 18 July 1920)

The surrounding sense world, excluding ourselves, is thus not the immediate expression and activity of divine-spiritual beings but of lower supersensory beings which the gods have detached from themselves, and which they use to bring to manifestation their thoughts from the past. These are the beings of the world of the elements.

> By contrast, the relation of divine-spiritual beings to human beings is present and immediate; the gods themselves as living beings are active in us. The beings of the first hierarchy (Seraphim, Cherubim, and Thrones) operate essentially in the human metabolic-limb system; the second hierarchy (Spirits of Wisdom, Movement, and Form), in breath and pulse of the rhythmic system; and the third hierarchy (Spirits of Personality, archangels and angels), in the nerve-sense system. (GA 239, 5 June 1924, not quoted)

This present living activity of the gods in the human being is forming the seeds for a future nature and, when the time comes, will, as divine forces of the past, build the foundation for nature in the Jupiter existence.

> The actual creative gods are within human skin, in the human organs. In their being, humans are the bearers of the present divine-spiritual element. . . . That which imbues the whole human organism with spirit and soul, will continue to develop. . . . Divine-spiritual creativity, which holds sway in the present and will continue to do so into the future, is present inside the human skin, . . . only this will live over into Jupiter, this carries earth existence into its future planetary development. (GA 198, 18 July 1920)

Thus the human individual lives 'as a god-permeated being in a god-unpermeated world'. Only in such a world, devoid of gods, could humanity 'advance from a dim consciousness to bright, free self-awareness, to its own free intelligence and free will. (GA 26, Christmas 1924)

The various regions of spirit land are related in specific ways to each other and also to the lower worlds. In the lowest region—referred to in *Theosophy* as the *first*—there arise the archetypes of all *physical* forms.

> The first region contains the archetypes of the physical world inasmuch as these are not endowed with life. The archetypes of the minerals are to be found here—and also of the plants, but only in as much as they are purely physical, so to the extent that we disregard the life in them. Likewise, we also meet here the animal and human physical forms. (GA 9, *The Three Worlds III*)

Everything that appears on the physical plane in sense-perceptible form is a condensed image of what is pre-figured as thought-form in this first region of the world of archetypes.

> Imagine a certain space filled with all sorts of physical bodies. And now think these physical bodies away, and in their place think of hollow spaces with the shape of the bodies. Now imagine the previously empty space *between* the bodies full of the most manifold forms which have connections to the previous bodies in a multiplicity of ways—this is roughly how it looks in the lowest region of the world of archetypes. The things and beings embodied in the physical world exists in this region as 'hollows'. And it is in the spaces in between them that the mobile activity of the archetypes takes place. In the process of physical embodiment these hollows are filled up, so to speak, with physical substance. Someone looking at the space simultaneously with physical and spiritual eyes can see the physical bodies and between them the mobile activity of the creating archetypes. (GA 9, *The Three Worlds III*)

From these last words it is clear that we should not think of the world of archetypes—or indeed of the supersensory worlds in general—as existing in unimaginable distant heights, but as permeating our sense world. Everything which, at the physical level, consists of solid mineral substance not artificially manufactured by human activity, also exists negatively, as a hollow, in this first region of spirit land. 'Curiously this is the case only with things of nature, whereas man-made objects are positive in Devachan.' (GA 94, 1 July 1906)

In the *second lowest* region of spirit land are generated the archetypes of *life*, whose bearer is the ether, particularly the light-ether.

> Life here is a complete unity. It flows through the world of spirit as a fluid element, pulsating as though like blood through everything.... Flowing life formed of thought substance: this is how we could describe this second level of spirit land. In this element lie the primordial creative forces for everything that manifests in physical reality as a living being. (GA 9, *The Three Worlds III*)

Through the etheric body the physical forms of plants, animals, and human beings are imbued with life forces, that is, with the capacity to change from within, to grow and bring forth new forms of the same kind. To supersensory sight the etheric body also appears in a definite, albeit constantly changing form. The archetype for this configuration of the etheric body of earthly beings arises in this second region of the land of spirits.

The *third* region of spirit land contains the thought archetypes of the *soul element*, that is, of the astral beings and forces that are the bearers of soul life. 'Everything that goes on in souls in the two other worlds has its spiritual counterpart here. All sensations, feelings, instincts, passions and so on, are present again here at a spiritual level.' (GA 9, *The Three Worlds III*) What manifests as human soul-experiences on earth, and what also finds corresponding expression in the animal world, is present in the soul world as soul-astral formations, and can be seen there as such by the seer. 'Everything that a person thinks, experiences and feels, lives in their astral aura as a form, as a thought- or sentience- or feeling-form.' (GA 113, 25 August 1909)

The astral body also has a specific form. 'The astral body is the outer form for all soul content, for passions, emotions, drives, desires, feelings of pleasure and displeasure, enthusiasm, and so on. It appears in the most diverse shapes.' (GA 93a, 5 October 1905) The archetypes of all these soul-structure forms, and also of the astral body, are generated in this third region of spirit land. Thus archetypes are formed in these three lower regions and then condense in the lower worlds to soul{/astral}, etheric, and physical formations.

About the archetypes in the *fourth* region of spirit land, *Theosophy* says the following:

> The archetypes of the fourth region are not directly related to the lower worlds. In certain respects they are entities that govern the archetypes of the three lower regions, and mediate their co-ordination. Thus they are occupied with the ordering and grouping of these lower-level archetypes. Accordingly this region exercises a more comprehensive activity than the lower ones. (GA 9, *The Three Worlds III*)

In this fourth region the creative thought seeds take shape as thought beings integrating the three lower-region archetypes into the manifold thought archetypes that appear in the soul, etheric and physical world as formations combined from many separate elements. This region thus plays a mediating role between the thought seeds of the higher spirit-realm divisions and the thought archetypes of the lower ones. The thought beings of the fourth region permeate the lower regions, ordering and grouping them.

> Just as warmth permeates our three lower regions, so there is also a common element that permeates the three [lower] regions we mentioned of Devachan. And what permeates everything there is the substance of our thoughts which live there as forms and beings. Here are the beings that permeate the whole space of Devachan like gradations of warmth. (GA 109, 6 June 1909)

Also in this fourth region of spirit land are generated the thought forms which, as 'pure' thought, weave within themselves, that is, have no direct connection to archetypes of the lower regions or to concrete soul and physical phenomena. In other words, when a human being thinks about things of the sense world, such thoughts are a shadow image of archetypes from the three lower regions of spirit land. When, on the other hand, a person thinks sense-free thoughts, which are not an image of anything already there, such thoughts are the shadowy reflection of archetypes of the fourth region. Thus all creative thought of human beings, through which something new is incorporated into the world, has its origin in this fourth region. The thought forms of all original ideas that arise from within the human being, through which, for example, works of art, machines and suchlike are created, are prefigured in this region.

> We can see that, as described, the three [lower] regions of spirit land have a particular relation to the worlds below them, to the physical and soul world. For they contain the archetypes, the living thought beings, which take on bodily or soul existence in these worlds. The fourth region is the beginning of 'pure spirit land'. But it is not even this in the fullest sense of the word. It differs from the three lower regions in that in them are to be found the archetypes for those physical and soul relationships which human beings find 'ready-made' in the physical and soul world before they intervene.... But through human individuals there have come into the world the creations of the arts, sciences, technology, the state, and so on: in short, everything that human beings incorporate into the world as the original works of the human mind. Without human participation there would be no physical images of all this in the world. The archetypes for these purely human creations are in the fourth region of spirit land.... We should not imagine that this fourth region of spirit land has significance only for outstanding individuals; it has significance for *everyone*. Everything that occupies people in physical life beyond the sphere of everyday life, wishes and wants, has its origin in *this* region. (GA 9, *The Three Worlds IV*)

The archetypes of creative human thought of this kind arise in the fourth region of spirit land through thought seeds of the higher regions. 'The ideas through which the human mind appears creatively in the physical world, are the reflection, the shadow, of these seed-thought beings of the higher spiritual world.' (GA 9, *The Three Worlds III*). This higher spiritual world is the region from which:

> ... the eternal aims of gods bestow
> Light of world existence
> on the individual 'I'
> for free willing...
>
> (from 'The Foundation Stone', GA 260, 25 December 1923)

The fourth region belongs to both the higher and lower spirit realms at the same time. Just as, in the physical world, warmth passes from the state of warmth-ether to physical warmth, so we can imagine thoughts in this region passing directly from a formless into a formed condition. To the extent that the archetypes here of creative human thought originate in the thought seeds of the higher regions, we can regard this fourth region as belonging to 'pure spirit land'.

The *three higher* regions of spirit land contain the thought-seed forces of the physical, life, and soul elements. The highest region, the *seventh*, is the origin of the germinal power of the physical realm in so far as this is expressed in the sense world as the unformed mineral materiality of all that is fluid, gaseous or warmth-related. When these seed forces of the seventh region unite with the shaping forces of the physical element of the lowest, the first region, the thought archetypes then arise here which condense into the physical-mineral formations of the sense-perceptible world. The second highest, the *sixth* region is the seat of the thought-seed forces that are the bearers of *life*. Through these the thought archetypes are produced, in the second lowest region, whose etheric image maintains the life of all earthly beings. To the *fifth* region of the spirit realm belong the thought-seed forces which create, in the third region, the archetypes of the organs that bear the *soul life* of animals and human beings. And what appears in humans as spirit {or mind}, that is, as pure thought, originates in the thought beings of the *fourth* region. This gives us the following divisions of spirit land:

7th region:	thought-seed forces for what is physical
6th region:	thought-seed forces for what has life
5th region:	thought-seed forces for what has soul
4th region:	thought-seed forces and thought-archetypes of what is spiritual {or purely mental}, the thought itself.
3rd region:	thought archetypes for what has soul
2nd region:	thought archetypes for what has life
1st region:	thought archetypes for what is physical.

Thought seeds of the highest region are structured and shaped in thought in the lowest region; those of the second highest, in the second lowest; and the third highest, in the third lowest. The fourth region stands alone as a connecting mid-point. This interplay and counterplay of thought forces shows again the law of cyclical relationships: the law whereby higher levels are repeated at lower levels within a sevenfold structure; the higher worlds create a mirror-image of themselves in the lower worlds.

To the three higher regions of spirit land also belong the rudimentary beginnings of man's higher members-of-being,* which he will develop as

* Translator's footnote: *members-of-being,* a more or less direct translation of the German *Wesensglieder,* is the hyphenated phrase I have chosen to serve as a technical, overarching term for all the levels, members, sheaths, or envelopes that make up the human and higher beings. It is useful in that it includes not just the 'bodies' but also soul and spiritual levels—thus, for example, 'astral body', 'consciousness-soul', and 'spirit-self' are arguably not all subtle bodies, but they are all members-of-being.

his own possession only during the future embodiments of the earth, but which, filled with forces of divine-spiritual powers, already work into the human being from higher worlds. Without them the lower human members-of-being could not exist.

> What he [the human being] actually is as a spirit in spirit land, only becomes apparent when, in the period between two incarnations, he ascends into spirit land's fifth region. What he is here is truly himself. . . . In this region the true self of the human being can express itself freely on all sides. . . . We see that what in this book is termed *spirit-self* lives in this region, to the extent that it has developed, in the reality appropriate to it. (GA 9, *The Three Worlds IV*)

Spirit-self is the transformed, spiritualized astral body, which is the bearer of soul life. And the fact that spirit-man, the spiritualized physical body, is assigned to the highest, the seventh, region, also follows from *Theosophy*. For when the human being experiences himself in his spirit-man, he has reached 'the farthest border of the three worlds'. And life-spirit, the transformed etheric or life-body, has its seat in the second highest region of spirit land, the region of the thought-seed forces of life.

In his descriptions of the spiritual world, Rudolf Steiner uses terms by which he compares it with the states of matter in the sense world, but which at the same time point to the connections existing between the worlds. He calls the lowest level of spirit land, which contains the archetypes of the physical, the *continental* region of spirit land; the second region, the archetypes of life, he calls the *oceanic* region; and the third region, the archetypes of the soul element, he calls the *atmospheric* region. The first region corresponds with the Mars sphere, the second with the Jupiter sphere, and the third with the Saturn sphere. The four higher regions of the spiritual realm lie beyond our planetary system in the worlds of the fixed stars. (GA 14, 1 February 1913, not quoted)

The substance in the three higher regions of spirit land, on the arupa plane, is only formless at the beginning of an evolution, holding all formations in a germinal, potential condition. By passing through successive earth lives, the human being carries the fruits of these lives into the arupic realms and impresses them into the formless substance of these regions so that they are gradually filled with forms which develop and shape the higher human members-of-being into spirit-self, life-spirit and spirit-man.

> The arupa plane in itself is formless but becomes formed through human lives. The human being gathers lessons on the physical plane

> and carries these up to the arupa plane. Accordingly, in Greek esotericism the soul was called a bee, the arupa plane a beehive, and the physical earth a flower meadow. This was taught in the mysteries. (GA 93a, 6 October 1905)

> Initially Devachan is short. But gradually, more and more, spiritual organs are developed in the mental body until finally, when he has encompassed the wisdom of the earth, the human being has developed and formed the Devachanic body completely.... There is no other way for human evolution to awaken the organs for Devachan than spiritual activity on the physical plane. (GA 93a, 9 October 1905)

What is said here about the mental body (spirit-self), applies likewise to the later development of life-spirit and spirit-man.

These forms, taking shape in Devachan as the product of human development in the lower worlds, appear here again in seed condition.

> The human being must refine himself completely, so that finally only a seed, a germinal condition remains of everything he has absorbed. In the end, all experiences are then concentrated as energy, as though in a point. The seeds that existed in the first Globe did not yet contain this. But in the final Globe the seeds hold everything they have experienced throughout the successive Globes. (GA 93a, 26 October 1905)

Thus everything proceeds from arupa as formless seed, and returns to it as formed seed. Just as, at the beginning of our evolution, these seeds were filled with the forces of divine creative powers, so at the end of our creation cycle they will contain the Christ-imbued spiritual striving of human souls as forces for the future from which a new world system can arise. The human being will then have advanced from creature to creator.

3. The elementary kingdoms as form-creating thought-seed beings and as the shaping forces of the kingdoms of nature

As we saw in the last chapter, the three higher, arupa-plane regions of spirit land contain, as thought-seed entities, those forces by which all forms of manifestation in the lower worlds are brought about. And it is these still-formless, living thought beings of the higher spirit region that Rudolf Steiner, in his book *Theosophy*, calls the three elementary kingdoms. *Thus the elementary kingdoms are the form-creating thought-seed beings of the arupa plane*, which give everything that is shaped (and appears in the world of archetypes, in the astral, etheric, and physical worlds) its supersensory or sense-perceptible form.

The *first elementary kingdom* consists of the formless thought-seed beings of the highest, the seventh region, of spirit land, which give rise to what is *mineral and manifested in physical form*. We must distinguish between the essential being (the mineral) and the physical form in which 'minerality' manifests. 'We must make a distinction between "physical" and "mineral"; they are not the same. Because today the physical and mineral appear to coincide, it is easy to confuse them.' (GA 104, 27 June 1908)

'A physical body is one that is governed by physical laws. The present human physical body is not only governed by these physical laws but in addition is permeated by mineral matter.' (GA 13, *Occult Science*, chapter: 'Saturn evolution')

The mineral substance of physical formations is subject to a constant process of dissolution and renewal, a constant streaming from within outwards. The mineral constituents, for example of the human physical body, renew themselves completely every seven years or so. Matter is exchanged, the spiritual form remains. (GA 235 25 January 1924, not quoted)

> The actual mineral kingdom has been added during the earth epoch, and what makes up the sense-perceptible world of the physical plane is completely impregnated by the mineral element. You don't see anything in plants, animals or people but the minerality with which they are impregnated. We only see what is mineral, earthly. (GA 254, 17 October 1915)

> We meet this physical world in its most characteristic form only where it is mineral kingdom. By staying in the mineral kingdom in the widest

> sense—naturally including water, air, and heat phenomena, the phenomena of the warmth-ether—we can study the forces, the essential nature, of the physical world. (GA 214, 28 July 1922)

The phenomena of the sense world arise through the connection of the essential being of the mineral with physical formative forces. In itself the mineral element is outwardly just as imperceptible as the physical. The fact that we perceive the sense world as such is a consequence of the luciferic temptation through which our 'eyes (i.e. sense organs) were opened'. But they were opened in such a way as to transmit a false picture of the physical world by concealing the spirit manifesting in it.

Both the physical, as form-principle, and the mineral element, as existential being, have their origin in the highest region of spirit land, and pass from there through all the Stages of Form. 'The physical can also exist in such a way that externally it has the form of ethericity, indeed even of astrality. A distinction must be made between the outer appearance and the inner laws. Something physical can etherize and astralize itself, and yet retain the physical laws.' (GA 13, *Occult Science*, chapter: 'Earth evolution') The same holds true for the mineral:

> The mineral kingdom passes through all the Stages of Form. Its foundations as mineral kingdom can be laid down in the highest levels of Devachan. It then descends into the lower spiritual levels but is still mineral kingdom, then to the astral level where it is pre-figured astrally, and then it condenses to the physical level. (GA 104, 27 June 1908)

> Just as ice is only one form in which water can exist, so the things of the senses are only one form in which beings of soul and spirit exist. Once one has understood this, one can also comprehend that, just as water can turn into ice, so the spirit world can transform into soul world, and soul world into sense world. (GA 9, *The Three Worlds V*).

The essential nature of the mineral has the tendency at the physical level to take on crystal form. 'When we look at the most characteristic form of the mineral, we have the crystal form.' (GA 208, 5 November 1921) 'Actually, we must look for crystals in all substances. And the substances we find that are not in crystalline form, that are formless like dust and the like, are really destroyed crystallizations.' (GA 220, 13 January 1923)

Behind all physical-mineral structures lies a supersensory energy form {or form field}. This *form body*, which holds the mineral substances together, is the real physical body; it is shaped by the forces of the first elementary kingdom. This applies not only to crystals, but to the physical bodies of plants, animals, and man.

> If you go to the very lowest boundary of the human organism you would have to think of the very highest supersensory entity, the human form which, as a system of forces born out of supersensory worlds, is destined as a ... super-physical, supersensory entity to absorb what causes the human being to appear physically to the senses in the first place. Only by the incorporation of food matter into this superphysical form does the human organism become a physical sense-perceptible one, one which we can see with our eyes and touch with our hands. We call what is presented in this way to the external food substances a *form* because actually in all nature there works a law, ... which is everywhere called the *form principle*. We can look down to the level of the crystal, and must say that, in order for a crystal to appear as it does, the substances that go into it must be captured, as it were, by form principles. In crystals these are the principles of crystallization. (GA 128, 28 March 1911)

This supersensory body of form or force field—the physical body in the true sense—is called by Rudolf Steiner the *phantom*.

> This phantom is the pattern of the human form which, as a spiritual structure (*Geistgewebe*), works on the physical substances and forces so that they are absorbed into the form we find as the human being on the physical plane.... Just as a sculptor must have a *thought* which he impresses into his sculptural medium, so there also exists a thought of the human body, ... a real thought in the external world: the *phantom*.... What was developed throughout the Saturn, Sun and Moon epochs is the phantom, the form of the physical body. (GA 131, 10 October 1911)

In *Occult Science,* the first rudiments of the human physical body that were already taking shape on {Old} Saturn are likewise called human phantoms. This phantom of the human being as spirit-form is an image of the thought archetype of the human physical body that was created by the mental formative forces of the first elementary kingdom in the lower spirit region. A supersensory system of forces of this kind is not only behind the physical body as a whole, but also behind each individual physical organ. Certain elemental beings, whose body is subject to physical laws, are also called phantoms by Rudolf Steiner.

In giving form, the forces of the first elementary kingdom, by which the physical realm is formed, reach the limit of their powers; the mineral structures they create when working alone lack the capacity to change their form from within: they lack life.

The *second elementary kingdom* consists of the formless thought-seed forces of the second highest region of spirit land, the region of the thought seeds of life. They give shape, in the second lowest region, to the archetypes of life in all that is plant-like. Just as it is necessary to make a distinction at the physical-mineral level between form and the filling out of the form with mineral substance, so here the distinction is between the essential being of the plant and the vegetative organs through which it lives. It is these organs that are formed by the second elementary kingdom. The bearer of life forces is the etheric body, which also has a definite supersensory form, albeit one that is constantly changing. The German term *Leib* points to this.* 'The term *Leib* (living body) is used to indicate that which gives a being of any kind *shape* or *form*. We must not confuse the term *body* with the sense-perceptible bodily form. In the terms of this book, *body* can also be used to mean that which gives form at a soul or spiritual level.' (GA 9, *The Being of Man IV*)

The plant is thus acted upon by two elementary kingdoms: the first, building the physical form of the plant, and the second, endowing this form with life and keeping it flexible. When working alone, the germinal forces of the first elementary kingdom operate from the arupa plane. They are thus able to produce only fixed physical forms that cannot change. The germinal forces of the second elementary kingdom 'descend' so to speak to the rupa plane, and from here give shape to the archetypes of everything that is vegetative. By joining here with the arupa-plane germinal forces of the physical, which they draw along with them, as it were, to the rupa plane, the shape-creating germinal forces of the physical retain their shaping capacity. Thus there arise, in the second lowest region of spirit land, archetypes of the plant that are capable of change, that can continually bring forth new forms which the plant develops successively on the physical plane through stages from seedling, roots, stem, leaves, flowers and fruits to new seedling.

> The plant has within it the power to give itself its own living form and to reproduce this form as another creature of its own kind. . . . But there is also a form-endowed spirit-seed in plant life. But in this case the being that has been given form has retained the capacity to form. In crystals the spirit-seed, once shaped, loses its formative power. It has expressed itself completely in the created form. The plant also has form, but in addition it retains the capacity to create form. The attribute of the spirit-seeds in the higher regions of spirit land is preserved in plant

* Translator's footnote. *Leib* means 'a living body', as distinct from the more material word *Körper* 'body'—as in *Etherleib* 'etheric body', and *Astralleib* 'astral body'.

life. The plant is thus form, like the crystal, but also formative power. (GA 9, *The Three Worlds III*)

In crystals we find the transition from the formless mineral world {e.g. water, air, and heat, which are formless} to the living formative power of the plant kingdom. In this externally perceptible formation process—in both the mineral and plant kingdoms—we see, now condensing at the sense-perceptible level, the purely spiritual process which is at play when the spiritual seeds of the three higher regions of spirit land take shape as the spirit-forms of the lower regions. (GA 9, *The Three Worlds V*)

The beings of the second elementary kingdom are also at work in the vegetative aspects of animal and human nature. As described, they work in unison with beings of the first elementary kingdom, keeping flexible their formative forces of physicality. 'In this [human] physical body, beings are continually working from the highest regions of Devachan. And on the etheric body beings are continually working from the lower regions of Devachan.' (GA 103, 23 May 1908)

The mineral kingdom appears in a completely different way in the bodies of plants, animals, and man, than it does in crystals. This is because the etheric body, astral body, and Ego tear the mineral substance away from its physical existence, transform it and raise it to higher levels. As mentioned above, the mineral element can exist at etherized and astralized levels.

Plant life is possible on the earth because there are earthly substances which do not remain subject to physical laws but which, laying aside all physical law, take on other laws that are their opposite.... We can only understand the generation of the plant world when we see in it the working together of earthly-physicality and cosmic-ethericity.... When we follow the substance nature of earthly matter into formations of the ether, we must say: Wherever matter enters this {etheric} formation, it takes on a nature whereby it alienates itself from physical laws.... Physical matter undergoes a further development of its nature when it passes over into the weaving and life of the etheric.... [E]arthly matter must also flow into the astral body. It thereby estranges itself even more from its physical nature.... And again we become aware how earthly matter, by adapting itself to the weaving and being of the Ego, estranges itself yet further from its physical nature. It is of the utmost importance to realize that the ordinary human forces of thought are the refined forces of growth and form. (GA 27, Chap. 1)

The forces of physical form, the forces of the first elementary kingdom, also adapt themselves to this transformation of mineral substance through the supersensory members-of-being. They are torn away from physical existence and their activity transposed into etheric, astral, and spiritual levels. '... because in the human being the physical aspect is clothed in etheric, astral and Ego-nature, all of which change the physical, all of which adapt the physical to themselves, whereas in external physicality, in the mineral world, we meet this physical element unpermeated by etheric, astral, and Ego elements.' (GA 208, 5 November 1921)

Just as the formative forces of the first elementary kingdom are at work in pure minerality at the physical level, so in the plant they work at the etheric level, in the animal at the astral level, and in the human being at the mental-spiritual level—but always with the physical laws corresponding to their nature. This means that the mineral substance in plants, animals, and human beings, in its transformed condition, is still shaped by the formative forces of the first elementary kingdom. The physical form is *determined* by the supersensory members-of-being, but is *formed* by the forces of the first elementary kingdom. All this shows once again just how complicated the formative processes of the world are, and how essential it is for an understanding of them to be conscious of the multiplicity of phenomena involved, and of their interconnections.

The *animal* not only has form and life like the plant but is also ensouled with sensations, drives and instincts. The very different nature of the animal form in comparison with the plant already points to the working of higher formative forces here. The animal can move about freely; the plant is fixed to the spot. Internal and external organs give the animal the ability to satisfy its drives and desires. All these soul forces operating in the animal come to expression in its form and organism. Thus we find in animals a third type of thought-seed entity belonging to the fifth region of spirit land, the region of thought seeds for soul life. These thought seeds give form, in the third region, to the archetypes of *soul phenomena*. The astral body and its organs are formed according to these soul-phenomena archetypes. The astral body too 'appears in the most varied forms'. These thought-seed entities of the soul level, working in animal and man, comprise the *third elementary kingdom*. This kingdom takes the thought-seed forces of both the first and second elementary kingdoms, and draws them with it from the arupa plane to the soul-astral world. It is thus able to keep the soul forms it creates flexible and alive. Thus the higher elementary kingdoms always contain the form-creating forces of the lower ones.

> In the animal form the capacities of growth and reproduction are added to by those of sensation and drive. These are expressions of the soul world.... The plant cannot go further than its ability to create form; it constantly produces new forms during its life.... The animal has a finished form, and within this it unfolds and encloses a fluctuating life of sensation and drives. And this life has its existence in the soul world. So, just as the plant is something that grows and reproduces, the animal is something that senses and has drives and instincts. It is these that, for the animal, are the formless element that is constantly unfolding new forms. Ultimately they have their archetypal processes in the highest regions of spirit land. But they operate in the soul world. Thus in the animal world, in addition to the invisible force entities which direct growth and reproduction, there come others which have descended one stage further, into the soul world. In the animal kingdom there are formless entities which clothe themselves in soul-astral sheaths, and these are the taskmasters who cause sensations and drives to arise. They are the real architects of animal forms. (GA 9, *The Three Worlds V*)

Here too we must make a distinction between sensation and drives as such, and the astral organs through which the sensations and drives can find expression. It is these organs as bearers of soul life that are formed by the forces of the third elementary kingdom. The physical and etheric bodies of the animal are likewise formed as an expression of this third elementary kingdom working through the astral body, the astral body using for this purpose the formative forces of the first and second elementary kingdoms. For, also in the animal, the form of both these lower {physical and etheric} bodies is determined by the astral body, but they are formed by the first and second elementary kingdoms.

In the fourth, the middle region of spirit land, formless thought-seed entities give shape to the archetypes of the spiritual-mental level, that is, of thought itself. Since, on earth, thought life manifests in the human being, we can regard these thought-seed entities as the *fourth elementary kingdom*, as the elementary kingdom of man. This works at the mental-spiritual level of the Ego.

> The human being, apart from the capacities mentioned with regard to plants and animals, is also equipped with those which elaborate sensation into mental representations and thoughts, and which govern drives by means of thought. Thought, which appears as form in the plant and as soul force in the animal, emerges in the human being as thought itself, in its own form. The animal is soul; the human being is spirit. The spiritual aspect has descended another stage deeper. In the

> animal it gives form to the soul; in the human being it has moved right into the material world of the senses. Spirit {or mind} is present within the human body of the senses. And because it appears in a sense-perceptible garment, it can only reveal itself as a shadowy reflection of its essential spirit being, as represented by thoughts. By means of the conditions of the physical organism of the brain, the spirit manifests itself in the human being.
>
> But the spirit has thereby also become the inner being of man. Thought is the form which the formless spirit entity assumes in the human being, just as it assumes form in the plant and soul in the animal. Thus man, in so far as he is a thinking being, does not have an elementary kingdom building him up from without. His elementary kingdom is at work within his sense-perceptible body. Only inasmuch as man is a being of form and sentience do elemental beings work in him in the same way as they do in plants and animals. But the organism of thought is elaborated in man right from within his physical body. In the human spiritual-mental organism, in the nervous system elaborated into the perfected brain, we have visibly and sense-perceptibly before us what works in plants and animals as an invisible force. This causes the animal to evince self-feeling, and the human being self-consciousness. In the animal, spirit feels itself as soul; in the human being, spirit knows itself as spirit, even if only—due to the physical conditions—as a shadowy reflection of the spirit, as thought. (GA 9, *The Three Worlds V*)

The power of thought in human beings on earth, the ability to have mental pictures and thoughts, thus has its origin in the thought forces of this fourth region of spirit land. In this region, {formless} thought-seeds of the higher regions change into formed thoughts, into thought-archetypes.

But in this fourth region, human beings also build the *archetype of their Ego-structure*, which Rudolf Steiner also calls 'thought-body' or 'Ego-organization', because this also appears as a form. And by means of this Ego-structure archetype, human beings create, in this fourth region, the archetype of their earthly form as the expression of a thinking Ego. It employs for this process the soul, life, and physical archetypes in the lower regions of Devachan, which it integrates here. For the thought forces of this fourth region have an ordering and grouping character. As a region of thought formation, this fourth region belongs to the higher spiritual realm, and as a region for structuring forms, to the lower.

With regard to the creation of the human form's archetype, Rudolf Steiner says:

> When man entered Devachan for the first time, he had already built in spirit an archetype of the human being, and this then condensed to physical man. Now, having been through many incarnations, he takes an extract of the past life with him, and in accordance with this then builds the archetype of a new human being.... Once built, the archetype always has the impulse to appear again on earth—this archetype which is actually man himself.... At present, man does not have the power to develop by himself the archetype created in Devachan. In this cycle of life man cannot yet direct his own reincarnation; he needs higher spiritual beings. (GA 109/111, 6 June 1909)

Thus in the fourth region of the spiritual realm, the human archetype forms an archetype of its physical body by means of the formative thought forces of the first elementary kingdom, and with the aid of higher powers in the lowest, the first region. It forms an archetype of its etheric body in the second region, using the formative thought forces of the second elementary kingdom. And in the third region it forms an archetype of its astral body with the formative thought forces of the third elementary kingdom. The archetypes thus created then condense to the lower members-of-being of the earthly human being.

Not only beings of the higher hierarchies but also other human souls who are karmically connected with the individual, work on creating his spirit-form, initially the form of the head.

To this germinal foundation of the head is then added, during the passage through the starry worlds,

> the spiritual foundations for the subsequent new body, for the chest and limbs.... And this is wonderful work, how one human being works on the other there, how this work takes place in harmony with the beings of the higher hierarchies, how work is done on the human head in a way that is like the creation of a whole world in itself. For, every human head ... is a wonderful world with countless details, and work on it therefore requires dedication from human souls who are connected with each other by destiny. To this also belongs the work of those beings of the higher hierarchies who, out of the mystery of the cosmos, understand how such a human head is to be fashioned.... And what can grow in us from this view of what happens to human beings between death and re-birth, is a human sense of responsibility. And this sense tells us that we must indeed strive very hard to be worthy of being a human being, when we measure the whole significance of human existence by the meaning

this work on man, between death and a new birth, has for the gods. (GA 231, 17 November 1923 evening)

After conception the thought archetype of the human form, woven by formative thought forces of the spirit realm, is carried as the shaping, formative energy structure (phantom), as the 'spirit germ', into the maternal body where, during the embryonic period, material substances and forces, and the forces coming from the line of inheritance, are incorporated into it.

Based on what is presented concerning the elementary kingdoms in his *Theosophy*, Rudolf Steiner summarizes the seven kingdoms of earthly existence as follows:

1. The kingdom of archetypal formless beings (first elementary kingdom)
2. The kingdom of form-creating beings (second elementary kingdom)
3. The kingdom of soul-astral beings (third elementary kingdom)
4. The kingdom of created forms (crystal formations)
5. The kingdom that becomes sense-perceptible in forms, in which however the form-creating beings are still at work (plant kingdom)
6. The kingdom that becomes sense-perceptible in forms, but in which additionally the form-creating beings and entities expressing themselves in soul-astral phenomena operate (animal kingdom)
7. The kingdom that becomes sense-perceptible in forms, but in which additionally the form-creating beings and entities expressing themselves in soul-astral phenomena operate, and in which the spirit itself takes shape, in the form of thought, within the world of the senses (human kingdom).

From this we see how the fundamental components of the human being living in the body are connected with the spiritual world. . . . The physical body comes about by the human archetype condensing to the point of appearance in the sense world. We can therefore also call this physical body an entity of the first elementary kingdom that has condensed to the level of sensory appearance.

The etheric body comes about because the form that has thus arisen is kept flexible by a being that is itself invisible, but whose activity reaches into the sensory realm. If we wish to characterize this fully, we must say: it has its origin initially in the highest regions of spirit land, then, in the second region, shapes itself into an archetype of life. As an archetype of life it operates in the sensory world.

> Similarly, the being which builds up the sentient soul-body [astral body], originates in the highest regions of spirit land. Then it shapes itself, in the third region of spirit land, into an archetype of the soul world, and operates as such in the sense world.
>
> The intellectual/mind soul, however, is structured by the archetype of the thinking human being. This archetype shapes itself, in the fourth region of spirit land, into thought, and works directly as such in the thinking human being, in the sense world. (GA 9, *The Three Worlds V*)

The human physical body is shaped by the same physical forces that give form to the minerals. The human etheric body is given its forms by the same forces that shape the organs of life in plants. And the human astral body is built up by the same forces that form the organs of soul in the animal. There are therefore three extra-human elementary kingdoms at work on these human members-of-being: the first kingdom in the physical body, the second in the etheric body, and the third in the astral body. Only in the Ego-structure, the thought-body, is the human kingdom itself at work—the fourth kingdom.

In so far as minerals attain their form from the first elementary kingdom, plants their organs of life from the second kingdom, animals their organs of soul from the third kingdom, and human beings the organs that bear their thought life from the fourth kingdom, we can say: minerals live in the first, plants in the second, animals in the third, and man in the fourth, the mineral, elementary kingdom. As discussed above, during the course of their evolution, beings pass through these elementary kingdoms. Man, too, once lived in the first elementary kingdom: during Old Saturn when he was at the level of the minerals. During the Old Sun period, in addition to his physical body, he received an etheric body and thus lived a plant-like existence in the second elementary kingdom. In the Old Moon phase, with the integration of the astral body into his being, he rose to the animal level, and therefore lived in the third elementary kingdom. And by being endowed during earth existence with the Ego-component, the human being entered the fourth kingdom.

Thus the beings and forces of the elementary kingdoms are the foundation for the becoming of all beings and worlds. Mysteriously hidden, shaping and forming, they live and weave in everything that the world of the senses presents to us in its beauty, wonders and riddles, and also in everything that manifests as an expression of the supersensory subtle bodies of earthly creatures. No true understanding of the world is possible without an understanding of the elementary kingdoms.

4. The entrance of the elementary kingdoms into earth evolution and how they appear to clairvoyant vision

When earth evolution in its present fourth Stage of Life began making its transition from the astral to the physical Stage of Form on the arupa plane, the seeds of the elementary kingdoms still rested in higher beings, still formed a part as it were of the the spiritual organism of these beings. More precisely: the beings of the first elementary kingdom lived in the archai; those of the second elementary kingdom, in the archangels; and those of the third elementary kingdom, in the angels. When during further development the transition was then made from arupa to the subsequent rupa stage, 'the Spirits of Personality [the archai] detached certain entities from themselves.... This is the first elementary kingdom.' The beings of this first elementary kingdom operate from the arupa plane. This is why they could not participate in the advancing densification of earth from the condition of formless thought seeds to the stage of formed thoughts (archetypes). They had to remain behind at the arupa stage.

During the transition from rupa to the astral stage, 'something similar detached from the Fire Spirits [archangels].... They comprise the second elementary kingdom.' This second kingdom—the kingdom of life—was brought down, carried by the consciousness of the archangels, from the arupa to the rupa plane, in order to work from here at the etheric-vegetative level. When the earth made the transition to the astral condition of Form, this kingdom had to remain behind at the rupa stage.

And finally, during the further course of evolution, from the astral to the physical condition of form, 'certain indefinite, image-like entities [detached] at the beginning of the physical Stage of Form from the Spirits of Twilight [angels].... These dependent, swirling emotions comprise the third elementary kingdom.' (GA 11, *The Life of the earth*) This third kingdom remained on the astral plane, and operates from there in the soul life of man and animal.

Just as the beings of the three elementary kingdoms lived originally in the beings of the third hierarchy, so the beings of the fourth, the spiritual kingdom, live in the human being. This fourth kingdom descended in man to the physical plane, and works in human beings in the formation of thoughts.

Once the beings {or entities} of the three elementary kingdoms had been extracted from higher beings, they remained as thought-seed entities but without any independence or consciousness of their own. However, they could now be used by the beings of the third hierarchy, from whose consciousness they had been released, as formative thought forces. Thus the archai work formatively at the physical level using the forces of the first elementary kingdom; the archangels work at the etheric level using forces of the second elementary kingdom; and the angels, at the astral level, using forces of the third kingdom. The human members-of-being too are formed by the third hierarchy using these elemental-kingdom forces. This is connected with the fact that these {higher} beings are at present engaged in transforming their own lower members-of-being into higher, spiritual members. The archai are engaged in the transformation of their physical body into spirit-man; the archangels, their etheric body into life-spirit; and the angels, their astral body into spirit-self. Hence their close relation to the corresponding members-of-being in man, which can be regarded as 'extensions' as it were, as parts, of the members-of-being of the higher beings in question.

> It is indeed the case that the physical form we receive through birth and lay aside at death comes from the realm of the archai. We therefore actually have our physical form by virtue of being embraced by a spirit of the archai realm, . . . who then takes back what he has lent us during life. . . . If we now consider the human etheric body, then also here we definitely cannot say that we own it in the fullest sense. With regard to our etheric body we are clothed in an extension of the realm of archangels; and its dissolution does not mean that it vanishes into nothing: rather, it goes back into the archangelic realm. The arch-angeloi in turn have a certain claim to it; they lower a part of their being, as it were, into the human realm and thereby constitute the human etheric body during its life. . . . Our astral body is also not entirely our own: it is an extension of angelic beings. . . . Our astral body too is like a garment for our being, out of the realm of the angeloi. (GA 205, 17 July 1921)

It is the form of our bodily members, brought about by the elementary kingdoms, that is given to us by the beings of the third hierarchy.

The elementary kingdoms as living thought beings belong to the higher spirit region. But, because they operate in the lower worlds, clothing themselves as it were in the substances of these worlds, they can also be perceived there as Imaginations. Hence the beings of the first elementary kingdom are described as consisting 'of undefined thought-substance, flowing along, condensing and dissolving again like clouds. One couldn't describe them as independent beings, but only as an irregular, general mass.' The beings of the second elementary kingdom appear as 'shadowy images or schematic patterns, similar to the images of a dreamy picture-consciousness'. The beings of the third elementary kingdom are also 'not independent, but are able to express energies similar to human and animal passions and emotions. These dependent, whirring emotions compose the third elementary kingdom.... These creations of the third elementary kingdom can be perceived [by the seer] as flowing light, flakes of colour, as smells, tastes and all kinds of tones and sounds. Nevertheless, all the perceptions of this kind must be thought of as spectral.' (GA 11, *The Life of the earth*)

The beings of the third elementary kingdom appear to clairvoyant sight in Imaginations of sense-qualities without material substance. The beings of the second kingdom also appear in a pictorial form, as thought forms. By contrast, the beings of the first kingdom lack any pictorial quality; they appear as points of energy which mass together and separate again like clouds.

Some further indications about the elementary kingdoms are to be found in a lecture from the year 1905:

> Think of a world in which sense-qualities stream through space but are not perceived on any definite forms. Think of clouds of colour wafting through the world, of tones sounding through the world, all our sense impressions filling space but without being attached to any form. Then you have the third elementary kingdom. There the elements of light and fire suffuse space.... When we see a thought-form it is a colourful cloud, a movement vibrating within itself.... The third elementary kingdom isn't irregular but a criss-crossing swirl of lines, everything the expression of beautiful forms that glow within themselves. They are like luminous bodies whirring through space and glowing from within.
>
> The tones that sound through space are ordered numerically. What is particularly noticeable is that right from the outset everything is related in a particular way, in particular relationships, to everything else.... This was called the measure of things. Everything was ordered according to measure, number, form. Think away the sense-qualities and think of the world filled with such thought-figures: that is the second elementary kingdom, which is the basis of the third. There [in the second elementary kingdom] we only have forms woven by thoughts, cosmic-etheric thoughts. The first elementary kingdom is difficult to describe. Let us suppose that at some moment we think the thought, for example, of a spiral, then the thought of a lemniscate. Now we put ourselves in the situation of having the *intention* to think

> this, before the form arises; so first the intention to think a spiral and then the intention to think a lemniscate. Think of a world full of such thought-seeds. This formless world is the first elementary kingdom. (GA 93a, 27 October 1905)

So here too the first elementary kingdom reveals itself to the seer as consisting of thoughts that do not yet have any kind of form or pictorial quality and are therefore difficult to describe. They are the still-undeveloped thought-seeds or seed-points of the arupa plane. The second elementary kingdom appears to clairvoyant vision in a somewhat more tangible form, in shadowy images, but not yet with any sensory qualities. These entities consist of the formed thought-substance of the world of archetypes, the rupa plane; they appear to the seer as lines and figures. In the third elementary kingdom we are now dealing with more condensed thought structures which clothe themselves, on the astral plane, with astral substance. As a result of this conjunction with the substances of the astral or elemental world, the third elementary kingdom can express itself in sense impressions which, however, must not as yet be thought of as adhering to physical-mineral substance, and therefore cannot be outwardly perceived.

> In these three elementary kingdoms, as you know, we are dealing with a living, weaving flow of colour; we are dealing with a weaving world of tone. We are dealing with what, here in the physical world, adheres in a certain sense to external, solid, material things, and in the elemental world weaves and floats freely; the flowing spirit expresses itself in this free floating and weaving in the same way that matter does here in physical colour, in physical tone. But just as physical matter, we could say, holds colour fast in fixed external contours, so the spiritual aspect of the elementary kingdoms bears along the flowing colours in currents, in waves, in a game that is ever-changing in manifold ways. Initially, this life remains unconscious and subconscious for earthly man. (GA 222, 12 March 1923)

Thoughts formed by human beings also clothe themselves in astral material on the astral plane. 'Every thought that goes out from you takes on form in the astral world. On the astral plane, thoughts are realities. Every thought that we put into the world takes on . . . astral substance. Accordingly, when we have a thought, this clothes itself with astral material, condenses to definite forms.' (GA 94, 29 June 1903) 'If we wish to generate a thought, we must trace the corresponding figure in astral space. . . . Then we conduct astral material along the figure.' (GA 93a, 27

October 1905) Thus we can imagine the elementary kingdoms as thought-seed entities flowing in the elemental world as {1} points of energy, {2} as thought-figures, or {3} as thought-forms, without independence and without impetus of their own for their activity. The formative forces of these thought-seed entities are used by the angels, archangels, and archai in order to create formed structures in the soul, etheric and physical world.

One of the transcripts preserving the few indications given by Rudolf Steiner concerning the elementary kingdoms contains the following remarks:

> The fourth elementary kingdom is the mineral kingdom which reflects back what it receives. The fifth elementary kingdom, the plant kingdom, not only reflects sensory qualities but reflects them inwardly enlivened; it reflects forms. The second elementary kingdom is the formative principle of the third elementary kingdom. The mineral kingdom as the fourth elementary kingdom is condensed out of the properties of the third kingdom. The plant reflects the form of the second elementary kingdom; in other words, it develops form out of itself. The animal kingdom also reflects back the intentions that lie in the first elementary kingdom. (GA 93a, 27 October 1905)

If we try to decipher these indications, we could say: the second elementary kingdom arises on the foundation of the first since it is through the second elementary kingdom that the still-formless energy points of the first are ordered together into the lines and figures of the world of archetypes. The first elementary kingdom is thus contained in the second, and this in turn in the third: for, the lines and figures of the second elementary kingdom are permeated by the third with astral matter. The second elementary kingdom thus gives the third the forms that are to be filled out with astral substance. In this sense, the second kingdom is the formative principle of the third.

The fourth, the mineral kingdom, arises from the third. The forces of the third elementary kingdom come to expression at the astral level in supersensory sense-qualities without materiality. The mineral kingdom 'receives', as it were, these supersensory qualities of the third kingdom, and 'its exterior throws them back', that is, reflects them outwardly by permeating the supersensory sense-qualities with mineral substance and thus 'condensing' the third-kingdom properties into structures that are perceptible in the sense-world. Thus 'the mineral kingdom ... is condensed out of the properties of the third elementary kingdom'.

The fifth, the plant kingdom, like the mineral kingdom, also 'throws back the sense-qualities [of the third kingdom]': it gives plants their exterior form, but reflects this back 'inwardly enlivened', that is, it also 'reflects the forms [of life] of the second elementary kingdom'. The living plant 'develops forms [of the second elementary kingdom] out of itself', by keeping them inwardly flexible—that is, alive.

The formative energies of the first elementary kingdom can go no further than the rigid formations of the mineral kingdom. In the plant kingdom, the formative forces of the first elementary kingdom do remain flexible, that is, capable of development; but they constantly produce only the same plant forms in metamorphosis. In other words, they go no further than repetition; for it is the law of repetition that applies in the etheric body of the plant. 'Forwards and backwards the plant is always only leaf.' (Goethe) By contrast, in its astral body, the animal shapes the most varied forms in its inner life: its drives, instincts, appetites and passions. These soul forces also come to expression in the animal's physical organs which are shaped by the formative forces of the first elementary kingdom. To this extent 'the animal also reflects back the intentions [which are formless but formative], that lie in the first elementary kingdom'.

The mineral kingdom reflects back the astral qualities of the third elementary kingdom; the plant kingdom, the second kingdom's archetypal forms of life; and the animal kingdom, the formless thought-seeds (intentions) of the third elementary kingdom. The higher kingdoms contain the lower ones.

In a lecture from the early period of his anthroposophical work, Rudolf Steiner points to the spheres of existence in which the elementary kingdoms live. He says there:

> When a being lives in sound, it is in the first elementary kingdom. When it lives in light, it is in the second elementary kingdom. When it lives in fire, it is in the third kingdom. When it lives in air, it is in the mineral kingdom. If we were to ascend to the first elementary formation, we would come to a realm of flowing sound, to the first elementary kingdom. Then, as we descended, we would come to a realm pervaded by flowing light-images: the second elementary kingdom. Then we come into a realm of flowing light-images permeated with warmth: the third elementary kingdom. Then a realm where forms take shape. First elementary kingdom: sound/tone. Second elementary kingdom: light. Third elementary kingdom: fire. Fourth elementary kingdom: air, the Ego shapes itself. (Quoted from: Ernst Hagemann, *Vom Wesen des Lebendigen*, Section E 'Elementarreiche—Naturreiche', Lübeck 1963)

With regard to the elemental levels, Rudolf Steiner says the following:

> If we were to go back to the first elemental form, we would be absorbed into the Word, into flowing sound. At the second elemental level we would change over into flowing light. The third elemental level would permeate us with warmth. Finally, at the fourth elemental level, in the atmosphere of the earth, we would see self-consciousness appearing, which enables the human being to say 'I' to himself. (GA 94, 11 June 1906)

These words are clearly pointing to the activity of the elementary kingdoms in the elements during the earth's passage through the elemental (astral) condition, when evolution had advanced to the elemental-water condition. Sound, light and warmth are to be understood here as elemental—that is, supersensory—conditions. As we shall see later, the first elementary kingdom acts formatively through life-ether; the second, through sound-ether; the third, through light-ether; and the fourth, through warmth-ether. Sound-ether is also called *form-ether* because, as bearer of the harmony of the spheres, it orders all existence according to number and measure:

> On {Old} Moon, water was permeated by sound and thereby brought into regular movement. The physical bodies of the beings on Old Moon were thus set into an inner quivering. Limbs and members take shape in the form, but fade away again. It is a forming and dissolving again of organs, an experiencing of patterns and rhythms. This ripens the bodies to take up astral substance into themselves. Such a striking of primal sound into the watery substance is expressed in the Bible as God ordering everything according to measure, number and weight. (GA 109/111, 8 June 1909)

The same process was repeated when the earth, in its early stages, passed again through the elemental-water condition. 'Thus the most manifold shapes and patterns were formed by the music streaming in from cosmic space, and the substances dissolved in the water obeyed the cosmic music and ordered themselves according to it.' (GA 102, 16 March 1908) When describing these processes, Rudolf Steiner used to refer to the Chladni figures produced by sound in powder.

Thus we can imagine that the first elementary kingdom embodied itself as it were in the elemental sound-ether of the second kingdom, whereby the thought-seeds (points of energy) of the first kingdom were rhythmically ordered together by sound into lines and patterns. Thus it is the 'flowing sound' of elemental sound-ether—in which the beings of the first elementary kingdom live—that activates the first beginnings of form-creation in elemental water. What arises in this way are not yet lasting forms, but forms that constantly dissolve and re-shape again. Other forces had to intervene to give the transient forms a certain permanence.

During the transition in the earth's evolution from the elemental (astral) to the physical Stage of Form, the higher elemental ethers developed out of the 'finest ether', the life-ether, in the following order:

Life-ether
Sound/tone-ether
Light-ether
Warmth-ether

From elemental warmth-ether there subsequently emerged physical warmth and the other physical conditions. (GA 11, *Beginning of the Present earth*)

Accordingly, the ether that arises after sound-ether is light-ether, through which the third elementary kingdom performs its formative work. Thus we can imagine how the transient forms—those that have arisen through the second elementary kingdom by means of 'flowing sound'—are elementally condensed to 'flowing light-images' by the third kingdom using light-ether. Thus the beings of the second kingdom live in elemental light-ether. There then follows a further densification of these flowing third-kingdom light-images, whereby they are permeated with warmth from the fourth kingdom. This gives rise to 'light-images permeated by warmth'. The beings of the third elementary kingdom thus live in elemental fire, just as those of the second kingdom live in light, and those of the first in sound.

All the formations that have so far come about have done so still at the elemental level; they are not yet 'sculpted forms', but pictures, Imaginations. Now follows the transition from elemental to physical-mineral existence, in which for the first time permanent forms can take shape. Warmth is the bridge between the elemental and the physical-mineral states. However, at the physical level, warmth never appears alone on earth but always connected with other physical states. Therefore 'sculpted forms' can only arise in the next-dense physical element: in physical air. Thus the fourth elementary kingdom lives 'in air' as in a 'realm where form takes shape': in the mineral kingdom. In this realm of physical-mineral air, an Ego can 'shape itself', that is, express itself in its first external shape as an air form.

The fourth elementary kingdom is the human kingdom. When the Elohim said, 'Let us create Man' (that is, the human physical form, since

Man as a soul-spiritual being already existed at that time as a warmth-etheric being in the surroundings of the earth, in 'Paradise'), and blew into him the living breath, the human being condensed from the elemental-warm to the physical-airy condition: the Elohim fashioned man as an air-form. 'As long as people do not decide to picture themselves physically at that moment [after the six days of Creation] as a human being of warmth and air, ...then so long will people not understand their own origin.' (GA 122, 24 August 1910)

Densification at the physical level proceeded from the airy condition to the physical-watery and to the physical-solid states. The elementary kingdoms again created the forms in this process, no longer now at the elemental level but at the physical level. The airy physical condition was brought about by the third elementary kingdom; the watery condition by the second; and the solid state by the first. Thus it is always the elementary kingdoms that bring about shape and form on all levels of existence.

5. The elementary kingdoms' formative forces as divine sacrifice

The question as to the origin of the forces laid down in the thought-seed substance in the upper regions of spirit land, and which, as elementary kingdoms, exert a form-creating activity in lower worlds, leads us initially to the beginning of our creation cycle, to the emergence of Old Saturn out of the 'fire-of-will' sacrificed by the Thrones. (GA 13, 'The Development of Man,' section on 'Saturn Development') The Thrones, or Spirits of Will, had, on a previous solar system, brought their development to a certain conclusion enabling them to perform the 'Great Sacrifice'. This consisted in bestowing the substance of their own being for the sake of cosmic development.

> Human thinking, and even human clairvoyance, can barely presume to look into the sublime evolution that the Thrones had to undergo before they were in a position to sacrifice what could form the first foundation of the human physical body. . . . Development consists in a being attaining more and more the capacity for sacrifice, until finally it is in a position to sacrifice its own substance and being, as it were, to experience it as the greatest bliss to bestow the matter and substance it has developed. . . . The Thrones on Saturn were at a level where they were able to pour out the substance they had made their own during their previous development. They themselves rose up thereby to a higher stage of development. (GA 112, 27 June 1909)

> Why were the Thrones able to render up from their own substance that which Saturn needed? Because the Thrones prepared themselves in a previous {cosmic} system, through seven conditions, just as our own solar system is doing now. What had been developed earlier in a solar system, can now work down from cosmic space and is itself able to give birth to, and create, a new solar system. (GA 110, 14 April 1909)

What the Thrones poured from themselves at the beginning of the Saturn development was 'matter' in the form of warmth substance, and namely the substance of their own physical body. 'The Thrones were able to trickle physical substantiality, warmth substantiality out of themselves.' (GA 110, 17 April 1909)

'The bodies on Saturn were formed from the bodies of the Spirits of

Will.' (GA 13) This physical 'matter' in the form of warmth substance, which flowed from the bodies of the Thrones and formed the sphere of Saturn, was the expression of the will principle, for 'what we call will, expresses itself etherically in what we call fire'. (GA 144, 21 September 1909) 'The fact is, namely, that the external physical body that has flowed out from the being of Old Saturn, out of the Spirits of Will, presents nothing other than *will* seen from outside. In us, the will acts as inner life coming from within. These words are chosen very exactly; they correspond very exactly to the nature of the matter.' (GA 121, 11 June 1910)

And fire is the original condition from which everything of a physical-material nature arises: from fire comes the airy condition, the watery, and the solid. 'So basically we have nothing but fire. Everything is fire; condensed fire. Everything is born of fire.' (GA 110, 12 April 1909, evening)

And fire is the manifestation of the sacrificial deeds of higher powers.

> Conditions of warmth are the outer physical expression—the outer sensory expression in general—of sacrifice. And everywhere in the whole world where we perceive warmth, that warmth is the outer expression of what is behind it. Conditions of warmth are the deeds of sacrifice of beings. Therefore, if we wanted to characterize warmth in a really true sense, we would have to say: cosmic warmth is the revelation of cosmic sacrifice or cosmic sacrificial deeds. (GA 132, 7 November 1911)

Even though the evolution of the solar system preceding our own may have taken place under very different conditions, nevertheless the basic principles of evolution were apparently the same as in the present cycle of creation. For, with regard to higher beings, Rudolf Steiner speaks of them as having members-of-being up to spirit-man and beyond, and often indicates that these beings have ascended through the same stages of development which it is man's task to ascend. He once mentioned a rank of beings that have a twelfth member as their highest principle. The lowest principle of these beings is life-spirit, the transformed etheric body, and their twelfth member is also an etheric body but of a nature even higher than life-spirit; it is in substance the same as the human etheric body, but evolved to higher perfection, so that this etheric body does not receive life, as human beings do, but pours out life into the cosmos. (GA 102, 27 January 1908, not quoted) Thus the beings above man have passed, in their pre-Saturn evolution, through stages of Consciousness, Life, and Form, and gradually developed their members-of-being. 'The Thrones had previously undergone evolution in other cosmic systems, . . .

and came to the point of changing from creatures to creators, from a position of taking to a position of giving. . . . [They too] had to be human at one time.' (GA 110, 18 April 1909, morning)

At the beginning of Saturn, the Thrones were at a stage of consciousness that the Spirits of Form have now, and which human beings will reach only on Vulcan. It is 'a high, creative [super-spiritual] consciousness'. (GA 11, 'The Life of Saturn') This consciousness is reached when a being has transformed its physical body to spirit-man, Atma; that is, it has achieved full mastery over its physical body.

> When the Ego is master over the physical body, when it overcomes the forces that pose the strongest resistance {that is, those of the physical body}, then the individual has in himself spirit-man or Atma. . . . Outwardly the physical body appears as just a physical body, but inwardly it is completely governed by the Ego and suffused by its bright glow. Here the physical body is both physical body and Atma. (GA 110, 13 April 1909, evening)

Accordingly, the Thrones had also gained mastery over their physical body and transformed it into spirit-man. Spirit-man belongs to the highest region of spirit land, to the region containing, in germinal state, all the formative forces of the physical. Here the physical-material principle is completely spiritualized again, transformed into the form of thought seeds. Thus we must think of the Thrones' physical body, offered up by them for the creation of the world at the beginning of our evolution, as existing in this thought-seed condition. The Thrones poured out this spiritualized substance of their physical body at the beginning of Saturn development. From this came about the highest region of spirit land, the region of thought-seed forces for the physical, from which proceeded all the subsequent development of Saturn and our whole cycle of creation. The substance of their physical body, offered up by the Thrones in germinal state, held all the forces of development and form of the physical level. These creative forces were the same as those which govern and shape the physical today. 'The laws that held sway in this planet of warmth [Saturn]—in other words, what brought about differentiation, what organized the interweaving processes—these were the same laws that govern the dense, solid mineral today.' (GA 122, 19 August 1910) It is the laws of the first elementary kingdom which then, as now, shaped physicality. Thus the formative forces of the first elementary kingdom of Saturn have their origin in the 'being-substance' offered up by the Thrones.

As stated in *Occult Science*, this being-substance, poured out by the

Thrones at the beginning of Saturn evolution, was still 'will without any definite properties', which 'expressed itself as a not-yet-organized substance of the Saturn body'. This means that the Thrones selflessly refrained from giving the substance offered up by them any of their own individual formative *impulses*; they gave only their formative *forces* from which something new could arise. This gave other beings the possibility, with help from divine-spiritual beings, to construct their physical garment from this basic substance—which was free of characteristics or tendencies of its own—in accordance with their own evolutionary impulses. In this way the beings of earth's evolution formed their physical aspect from the being-substance of the Thrones using thought-seed forces of the first elementary kingdom.

All subsequent states of 'matter' evolved from this spiritualized physical substance sacrificed by the Thrones. Initially the Thrones condensed thought-seed substance of physicality to the warmth of Saturn. On {Old} Sun, the Saturn warmth gave rise to aeriform substance; on {Old} Moon, to watery substance; and on earth, to solid substance. It was the Thrones themselves who transformed the Saturn warmth into these denser conditions.

> The Thrones hardened their fire to the gaseous condition during the Sun period. But it was also they who condensed this gaseous element to the watery condition during Old Moon. And during earth existence they condense their watery element still further, to the state of solidity.... Such a process, which to outer appearances we can follow as a process of densification, is actually only *maya*, the illusion of a condensing process. In this very condensing there is spiritual weaving and being, a spiritual activity. (GA 122, 22 August 1910)

These processes lying behind the densification of substances were presented by Steiner in his lecture cycle *Die Evolution vom Gesichtspunkte des Wahrhaftigen* (Evolution from the perspective of truth) (GA 132). The physical principle is the foundation that carries life, soul, and spirit in earth's beings. So there is something remarkable here: what from an outer perspective appears as the densest material and as the latest result of creation—namely physical matter—arose, when we look for its origin, as the first element of existence and from the highest and most rarefied spirit substance. Thus, in a sense, the Thrones are the creators of our whole cosmic system.

> Those esotericists who gave names to the creations of the Spirits of Will in our earth existence, called these spirits *Thrones* because they have

> indeed built for us the thrones upon which we, as on a firm foundation, are always supported, and on which all existence on earth, as though on its solid thrones, continues to find its footing. These ancient terms contain something worthy of immense respect, of immense veneration, which can fill all our feeling. (GA 122, 22 August 1910)

In a similar way in which the Thrones, by offering up their being, created the primary substance of physicality, so other hierarchical beings too, by sacrificing the substance of *their* being in subsequent evolutionary epochs, implanted into this primary substance—prepared for them by the Thrones—the formational forces of life, soul and spirit (mind). When evolution entered the Old Sun period, the Spirits of Wisdom were the ones who had matured to the stage of the 'Great Sacrifice'. They sacrificed from their own being the forces of their etheric or life-body for the progress of the world. Again it was the forces of the etheric body—that is, of life-spirit—spiritualized to the condition of thought-seed, that were poured out by the Spirits of Wisdom; they too could sacrifice their etheric body, as the bearer of life forces, only once they had gained full mastery over it by transforming it to life-spirit. Thus the life-bearing forces of the second elementary kingdom are founded on the being-substance of the Spirits of Wisdom.

> [The Spirits of Wisdom] had become capable of streaming substance from themselves just as the Thrones had done at the beginning of Saturn when they gave the material basis for the physical body. But the substance of the Spirits of Wisdom is *ether*; that is, wisdom with inner mobility and power; in other words: life. Man's etheric or life-body is thus an outpouring of the Spirits of Wisdom. (GA 11, 'Life of the Sun') The Thrones are mightier beings; they can trickle physical substantiality, warmth substantiality, from themselves.... The Dominions or Spirits of Wisdom can only sacrifice an etheric body, which is thinner. (GA 110, 17 April 1909) The substance of the etheric body flowed from [the Spirits of Wisdom]. Ever since the Sun period we have carried the substance of the Spirits of Wisdom in our etheric body. (GA 108, 8 August 1908)

It was not ether in a generalized sense—in its four modes as warmth-, light-, sound-, and life-ether—that was integrated by the Spirits of Wisdom into the evolution of the Sun. After all, Saturn had already consisted of warmth-ether, and sound- and life-ether only appeared later during the Moon and earth periods respectively. So it was *light-ether*, as the substance of their being, that the Spirits of Wisdom poured out into evolution during the Sun phase. Light-ether is the actual bearer of life force. 'For everything that lives on earth, light is an element of life.' (GA 122, 21 August 1910) Thus also our sun today is 'not only light, but the power for life.... Behind our earthly light lies life streaming down from the sun'. (GA 56, 26 Mar 1908) 'Life streams down to the earth from cosmic space and is captured by earth's creatures; it comes from the Spirits of Wisdom.' (GA 121, 11 June 1910) When the physical body was permeated with the etheric body, it attained the capacity to develop wisdom-filled inner quickening and mobility. The human being on Old Sun thus consisted of warmth- and light-ether.

Warmth constitutes the transition from the etheric to the physical condition. In the warmth of Saturn, physical and etheric were not yet separated from each other as was the case in subsequent planetary phases, since there were no other physical substances on Saturn for physical warmth to permeate. The warmth element wove within itself, as it were. 'Warmth is movement, but must be thought of as intensive movement, movement in which, in every part of space where warmth is found, there is a striving to bring material being into existence and to cause material being to vanish again,' (GA 321, 11 March 1920) Saturn warmth was both etheric and physical at the same time—etheric as a constant factor, and physical as a factor coming into being and passing away. 'The physical body [of Saturn] is a rarefied, thin, etheric warmth-body.' (GA 13) Only on Old Sun, when warmth was able to unite with the physical air element, did it appear as permanent warmth, just as on the other side the ether now appeared as the opposite of the physical. Air and light arise from warmth at the same time. 'It is always the case that, when warmth material condenses to air material, it rarefies on the other side to a finer condition, to light material.' (GA 98, 17 March 1908) 'Nothing arises one-sidedly in the world. Everything that arises has two sides. When light arises through warmth, there also arises on the other side a darkening, dark material. This is a very ancient spiritual-scientific teaching.' (GA 110, 12 April 1909) Thus the one cannot arise without the other. During the transition from Saturn to Sun therefore, the Thrones and Spirits of Wisdom had to work together. 'If the ground had not been prepared by the Thrones, the Spirits of Wisdom would not have been able to begin their work.' (GA 109/111, 8 July 1909)

Although it was also the Thrones who condensed Saturn warmth to Sun air, nevertheless the collaboration of the Spirits of Wisdom was also required. Thus, at the beginning of the Sun phase and following a brief repetition of the Saturn conditions, a part of the warmth substance was condensed, through the working-together of these two hierarchies, to an aeriform or gaseous state, while a part of the warmth-ether was simultaneously transformed into light-ether. Together with this, the portion of warmth-ether that was not transformed continued to exist, and the physical air was permeated by this unchanged physical warmth. The light-ether also included, hidden within itself, the part of the warmth-ether from which it had itself emerged. Therefore, at work in both the air and the light-ether were the forces of the first and second elementary kingdoms. All this took place to begin with on the arupa plane in the still-formless contemplation of the creative powers, bringing about the foundation of the second elementary kingdom in the sixth region of spirit land—the region of thought-seed entities of life.

Old Sun consisted of physical warmth and warmth-ether along with light and light-ether. In this 'inner weaving of light, warmth, and air during the Old Sun phase', the plant life of Sun developed in such a way that 'the laws that operate in our present plant kingdom, the laws that determine that a root grows downwards and a flower upwards—these laws assert themselves within the ancient Sun conditions in the elements of air and warmth ... so we must imagine conditions on Old Sun as flower forms flashing up like light.' (GA 122, 19 August 1910) It was the laws of the second elementary kingdom that formed plant nature on Old Sun and that work in the same way in the plant world of the earth.

The Spirits of Wisdom also refrained from imparting to their sacrificed etheric forces any developmental impulses of their own. They gave them as neutral, undefined forces of development with which other beings could form, according to the impulses of their own inherent forms, their etheric bodies and etheric organs as bearers of life. Thus humans, animals and plants formed their etheric bodies using these forces of the second elementary kingdom.

The air on Old Sun, even during the physical Stage of Form, was not yet outwardly perceptible like air on earth; it was air in elemental state. The elemental world is the world of etheric forces that are behind the present mineral-physical earth. It is divided into a lower section of elemental-physical forces of substance, and a higher one of elemental etheric forces. 'So we can describe the elemental existence of earthly phenomena like this: warmth is again the middle condition; then we have air, water, and solid as states of densification, and light-ether, sound-ether, and life-ether as conditions of rarefaction.' (GA 122, 20 August 1910) Old Moon and the early Life Stages of the earth also proceeded at the elemental level. It was only with the entry into evolution of the mineral element during earth's Lemurian period that the physical-mineral world emerged by condensing out of the elemental level. (See Part II, 'The Elemental World')

In the elemental existence on Old Sun, air and light were still interwoven so that Sun's air glowed inwardly. With the streaming in of the etheric body of the Spirits of Wisdom, 'the previously dark Sun-beings began to glow'. (GA 13, section on 'The Life of the Sun') In the present earth conditions, by contrast, the air is flooded with light from outside and is therefore no longer self-glowing.

The beings of the second hierarchy were also involved in another way in the progressive densification of the original mass of Saturn to the subsequent planetary conditions. Ancient Saturn consisted of an immense sphere of warmth whose circumference extended beyond that of our present solar system. The first condensing of this Saturnian sphere occurred through the agency of the Spirits of Wisdom, or Dominions.

> It is these Dominions who now press in from outside and compress the originally immense Saturn-mass so that it becomes smaller. The Dominions pressed in so long that this ancient Sun became the size of a cosmic sphere whose mass, taking the sun as the centre, you must think of as extending to {the orbit of} Jupiter.... And it is through the Virtues [Spirits of Movement] that the mass of Old Sun was {subsequently} compressed to the boundary marked by {the orbit of} present-day Mars. Mars is in turn the boundary stone for the size of Old Moon. (GA 110, 14 April 1909)

Accordingly, it would have been the Spirits of Form who collaborated in condensing and compressing the Moon conditions to those of earth.

During the *Moon* period the *Spirits of Movement* sacrificed from their own being the forces of their astral body, their spirit-self, which had been spiritualized to a seed condition. After a short repetition of the conditions of Saturn and Sun, the Spirits of Movement integrated these forces into part of the primary substance which had already been transformed and implanted with the formative forces of physicality and life. This part of the primary substance thereby became, as fifth region of spirit land, the germinal substance for the soul element, with the ability to form soul organs and an astral body as the bearer of soul life. Thus the third elementary kingdom arose during the Moon period from the sacrificial substance of the Spirits of Movement. Using the forces of this third elementary kingdom, human beings during the Moon period, and humans and animals during the earth period, shaped their astral body. Through the working-together of the hierarchies during the Moon period, the watery element emerged from physical air, and sound-ether from the light-ether. 'Now we know that as the Sun progressed to Moon, the conditions of the air condensed to those of water.... What we saw during the developments on Old Sun as cloud substance massing together, this now congeals to something denser, to "water" emerging on Moon, to Moon oceans.' (GA 132, 14 November 1911)

Finally, during *earth* existence, the *Spirits of Form* sacrificed from their own being—from their Ego-structure—the formative forces of their own Ego- and thought-formation, and imbued with them a further part of the primary substance already prepared by the other beings. As a result there arose, as the fourth region of spirit land, the thought-seed substance with which humans form their Ego-body or thought-body, and in which they can unfold their life of thought. The fourth elementary kingdom now becomes the bearer of this Ego-related spiritual substance. Life-ether develops from sound-ether, and the solid earthly element from water.

Thus the formative forces of the first elementary kingdom have their origin in the being-substance of the Thrones; those of the second elementary kingdom, in the Spirits of Wisdom; those of the third kingdom, in the Spirits of Movement; and the fourth, in the realm of the Spirits of Form. Each new elementary kingdom also bears the forces of those preceding it. Thus the original, neutral, undetermined primary substance of Saturn was imbued with the various formative forces which, as elementary kingdoms, are used by the beings on earth to structure their members-of-being. High, divine-spiritual beings sacrificed the forces of their own substance—attained over long aeons of evolution—for the progressive creation of the world. Thus what has been attained by beings in earlier cosmic times is woven into subsequent evolutions as formative forces for other beings to use as they follow their own evolutionary goals. And the beings who sacrifice the substance of their being on the altar of cosmic life, ascend thereby into a higher spiritual existence.

The Thrones and beings of the second hierarchy gave the *substance* for the structures of the human members-of-being, whereas the Spirits of Form brought about their actual *shaping*. These beings, as their name implies, give all phenomena their form. The Spirits of Form sent down from the surroundings of Saturn 'their life-giving juices into the warmth-mass of Saturn, and their own form, their image, was reflected in this warmth-mass. And these reflected images were the first foundations of the human physical body. Already on Saturn man was literally an image of his divinity.' On Old Sun 'further development occurs through the Spirits of Form. They no longer have need of an etheric or life-body; they give away their etheric body and thereby permeate the first physical foundations of man with the etheric body. The etheric body which human beings received on Sun, is initially formed from the etheric body of the Spirits of Form, a portion of the etheric body of the Spirits of Form.'

Likewise, on Old Moon, 'the [human] astral body only arose through the Spirits of Form sacrificing their astral body', and during earth existence they then sacrificed their Ego-structure 'and fructified humans with the foundation of their I, so that the I, as it appears on earth, is a fructifying force that flows out from the Spirits of Form'. (GA 102, 29 February 1908) As the Spirits of Form advance from stage to stage in their own development, they give away in turn each member-of-being they no longer need, for the progressive evolution of man.

6. The elementary kingdoms as the life kernels of the kingdoms of nature

The picture we have built up so far of the elementary kingdoms needs something more to complete it. We have got to know the elementary kingdoms as the living thought beings of the higher regions of spirit land which, as still-formless seeds, contain the forces that bring about shape and form in the lower worlds.

These formative forces of cosmic thought revealed themselves as the sacrificial gifts of high, divine-spiritual powers of creation. Filled with the formative forces of the gods, but otherwise lacking any defined or directed impulses for activity, they comprise the spirit substance of the arupa plane. These thought seeds, which exist here as intentions, aims, possibilities, must be taken up by other beings and formatively elaborated in the lower worlds, even as far as the physical plane. Other beings, in other words, must connect with these thought seeds, make their formative forces their own, inform them with their own shaping impulses, and with their help structure their members-of-being.

What the nature of these beings is, who clothe themselves as it were in thought-seed substance and make use of its forces, can be found in the indications given by Rudolf Steiner concerning the highest human member-of-being: spirit-man.

Spirit-man, the spiritualized physical body, belongs to the highest region of spirit land—the region of thought-seed entities for all physical phenomena—and here reveals itself to the seer as just such a thought-seed being. Concerning this human thought-seed being, we find in *Theosophy* the following:

> We must picture this thought-seed being as having a composite nature. Only the seed coating, as it were, is taken from the element of the thought world. This encloses the actual *life kernel*. Here we have reached the limit of the 'three worlds', for the kernel originates in still higher worlds.... Similar life kernels exist also for other cosmic beings. They have their origin in higher worlds and are moved into the three worlds in order to accomplish their tasks there. (GA 9, *The Three Worlds III*)

And later we read: 'The seventh region of spirit land leads to the boundary limit of the "three worlds". Here the human being finds the "life kernels". By reaching the boundary of the three worlds, the human being recognizes himself here in his own life kernel.' (GA 9, *The Three Worlds IV*) The eternal spirit-being of man, his 'true I', is revealed in this life kernel. Life kernels of this nature also exist for animals, plants, and minerals. As life kernels, human beings were jointly engaged from the beginning of their development—although initially with a very dull consciousness—in the creation and development of their members-of-being. Already on Old Saturn, human beings worked from the surrounding spirit world on their physical bodies.

> Down below, the cosmic globe of Saturn contained only what is in our purely physical corporeal nature; it {Saturn} was surrounded by an etheric-astral atmosphere, so to speak, in which the Egos were embedded. Human beings were indeed present on Saturn, but with a very, very dull consciousness. These souls had the task of keeping lively and in activity something down there which belonged to them. They worked from above on their physical body. (GA 99, 26 June 1907)

It was also the life kernels themselves that, towards the end of the Saturn development and with the help of the Thrones, created the first germinal foundations of spirit-man. 'Around the middle of the seventh Round of Saturn,...man has reached the stage where he can work unconsciously on his own material body *(Stoffleib)*. Through this activity of his own, man creates, in his complete dullness {of consciousness} in the Saturn phase, the first germinal foundation for actual spirit-man.' (GA 11, 'The Life of Saturn')

Both the physical body and spirit-man are founded and developed by the thought-seed forces of the highest region of spirit land. The life kernels must join with the forces of this region in order to work on the physical body and spirit-man. In the same way—in order to work on their etheric and astral body, and on the foundation of life-spirit and spirit-self—the life kernels of all the beings must, during the course of their development, unite with the thought-seed forces of the two lower regions of arupa, with the region of life, and of soul. This applies also to the life kernels of animals, plants, and minerals. By uniting with the thought-seed substance of the arupa plane, the life kernels become beings of a corresponding nature. Thus *the elementary kingdoms prove to be the life kernels or Egos of earthly beings in their connection with the thought-seed substances of the higher regions of spirit land.*

Rudolf Steiner also speaks of the beings of the elementary kingdoms as Egos and contrasts them as 'other Egos' with group Egos or group souls. 'These other Egos have by stages remained behind the human kingdom;

they comprise the hidden realms, the elementary kingdoms, that lie behind our physical world and work into it. On the astral plane you would find warmth wafting to and fro, fire of a kind that moves independently to and fro, and beings embodied in it, as we ourselves were on Saturn.' (GA 98, 4 December 1907) Minerals, plants, and animals are also on the way to reaching a human level. In ancient Egypt, 'by connecting the human form with animals and depicting this in pictures, they brought to consciousness the figures of intermediary elemental beings, who in the progressive creation of the world are on the way to becoming human, but do not appear at the earthly level. . . . Such intermediary elemental beings do exist.' (GA 26, 28 December 1924) In these intermediary beings the life kernels of the animal kingdom are at work as the third elementary kingdom.

In the highest region, the life kernels unite with the seed-substance of the physical level and become the first elementary kingdom; in the second highest, the sixth region, they unite with the seed-substance of life to become the second elementary kingdom; in the fifth region, with that of the soul level to become the third kingdom; and in the fourth region, with that of the spiritual-mental level to become the fourth kingdom. In the Saturn phase, the human life kernels worked as the first elementary kingdom on their physical body and on the foundation of spirit-man; in the Sun period, as second elementary kingdom on their etheric body and on the foundation of life-spirit; in the Moon period, as third elementary kingdom on their astral body and on the foundation of spirit-self; and in the earth period, as fourth kingdom, on their thought-body, the Ego-structure, and on their Ego as a thinking spiritual entity. A corresponding process applies to the life kernels of the animals, plants, and minerals, which entered evolution after man.

In the present phase of earth, we find the first elementary kingdom as the life kernels of minerals, which are at the first Stage of Life, and are connected with the thought-seed substance of physicality in the seventh region of the spiritual realm.

The life kernels of the plant, being at the second Stage of Life, unite with the thought-seed substance of life, and comprise the second elementary kingdom in the sixth region.

The life kernels of animals, at the third Stage of Life, are connected with the thought-seed substance of soul. These are the third elementary kingdom, in the fifth region.

The fourth kingdom is comprised of human life kernels at the fourth Life Stage. They are connected with the thought-substance of the fourth region of spirit land.

Thus, when looking at the elementary kingdoms, we are dealing with a twofold nature: with the life kernels, and with what enfolds them—the thought-seed substance.

We will look first at the life kernels.

6.1 Life Kernels

In his book *Theosophy* (GA 9), Rudolf Steiner refers to life kernels also as 'primal beings' and 'force entities'. In his work *The Akashic Chronicle* (GA 11), he refers to the predecessors of present human beings as 'force entities' (*Kraftwesenheiten*) which, during the Saturn, Sun, and Moon periods, themselves created, through their own activity with help from the beings of the first hierarchy, the first foundations of their higher members-of-being. He also refers there to spirit-man as the highest member of the 'so-called human monad'. A monad is 'the soul that bears itself through eternities, ... a being enclosed in itself and supporting itself'. (GA 138, 28 Aug 1912) This monad is the eternal core of man's being, who, once he becomes conscious of his self, can say to himself: 'I'.

> We live in three worlds: in the physical, astral, and mental world. Our existence oscillates between these three worlds. We have an inner core of our being, the 'monad'. We keep this inner core throughout the three worlds.... This inner core is always clothed there in a different garment.... Man is a dual being, composed of two aspects: of the monad and of the monad's clothing.... The monad has descended from the highest regions of Devachan.... At present man is fourfold. He has a physical body, an etheric body, and an astral body, and in these the Ego, the monad. (GA 93a. 24 October 1905)

Such monads exist not only for man but also for the other beings of the earth—for animals, plants, and minerals.

Monads have their origin in still higher worlds from which they descend into Devachan. For there are other spiritual worlds above Devachan to which man will ascend only after the Vulcan phase, but into which divine-spiritual beings already extend. The first of these worlds bordering on Devachan, on the spirit world, is the world of Foresight or the Buddhi plane; and the next highest above that is the plane of Nirvana. It was from this plane of Nirvana that human monads descended during earth's Lemurian period in order to unite with their life kernels.

> Man appeared on earth in the middle of the Lemurian period.... At that time there had to work down into the world something which came from Nirvana.... The beings that fructified the world at that

time had to extend right into Nirvana. What fructified the four-footed beings [the human-like beings of early Lemuria] so that they became human, were beings that descended from the plane of Nirvana. They are called monads.' (GA 93a, 11 October 1905)

In the Lemurian period a fourth member-of-being, the Ego-member, was added to the lower members-of-being, to the physical, etheric, and astral bodies, as far as these had been developed up to that point. At the same time 'a higher principle, the soul as an inner being' was integrated into this fourfold human nature. (GA 11, 'Fourfold Man') This soul as inner being, the earthly 'I' of man, is a reflection, an image in the earthly realm of the monad. It was now that man first appeared on the earth in the true sense. All the preceding humanoid creatures had not yet been human in this full sense, but a kind of pre-human. The human life kernels therefore were already preparing the development of the members-of-being at a time when the monads were still living on the plane of Nirvana. Thus the life kernels are again only an image, an instrument of the monads, just as the earthly Ego is similarly an image of the monad.

At their entry into evolution in the three worlds, the life kernels were placed by higher divine-spiritual beings into the highest region of spirit land in order to accomplish their passage through the stages of Consciousness, Life, and Form. During the early stages of their development, in the first three stages of life, the life kernels still have no independent existence or consciousness of their own. They are not yet separated into individual beings but form an undifferentiated mass like water drops in a body of water that are indiscernible and intermixed. We cannot therefore speak of individual beings here but only of a kind of general, overall being as the totality of the beings in question.

In this condition life kernels are still carried by higher beings through their successive evolutionary stages. What life kernels or primal beings 'do' is accordingly not strictly their own activity but that of the beings carrying them. These higher beings work through and with them while elaborating and developing the potential forces and capacities with which the life kernels have been endowed. We need to understand it this way when Rudolf Steiner speaks, for example, of the force entities working as 'taskmasters' in plant growth or in the sense impressions of animals. For the life kernels are endowed, right from their divine origin, with the seeds of all their later development, like the whole future plant in the plant seed. 'At that time, all things were present in the arupa Globe as the thoughts of spirits. What caused the gods to have in mind the thought of man? What was the model for this? It was the monads—which already existed but were not yet connected with man.' (GA 93a, 28 October 1905) Thus also for animals, plants, and minerals, it is the hidden characteristics predisposed in the monads of these other earthly creatures that give the gods the model for their work on these beings. Little by little, higher beings elaborate and develop the predispositions of the primal beings until, as the light of their consciousness progressively increases, they gradually become able to assume more and more of the work themselves.

This increase in consciousness goes hand in hand with a gradual primal-being separation. At the spiritual level the mineral kingdom is still a single unity. The archetype 'of the whole mineral world can be found as a totality in the spiritual world'. (GA 9, *The Three Worlds V*) The plant kingdom, and even more so the animal kingdom, do not present any sort of individual separation; they do however show a certain collective separation coming to expression in the various plant and animal genera and species. Only in the fourth Life Stage does the primal collectivity dissolve into individual Ego-beings. The primal beings now begin to have a consciousness of self, each one experiencing itself as an 'I', and as such joining consciously in the work on its development.

Thus the spirit-self of minerals, plants, and animals is still living a unified, dependent existence in group souls directed by higher spiritual powers. Only man, in his earthly Ego, has reached the first lighting up of self-consciousness. Yet the human kingdom is itself still reliant to a considerable degree on guidance from higher powers; in the further course of evolution our souls will increasingly work away from these towards full self-knowledge and independence. Man 'is only on the way to fully integrating his individual soul into his physical body. He will only have this completed individual soul once earth existence is more or less accomplished. ...For the vast majority of people today, their Ego is a half-way product between a group ego and an individual Ego.' (GA 101, 27 December 1907)

It is now apparent that the development of life kernels through the three worlds is such that the *unfolding of essential being* and the *formation of the bodily 'garments'*, take place on separate paths. So we need to imagine it as follows: The life kernels operate, as the instruments of the monads, under the direction of higher powers in a dual way. On the one hand, as elementary kingdoms using the seed-thought forces of the higher regions of the spirit realm, they form their 'garments' (that is, their members-of-being) out of the substances of the individual Stages of Form. On the other hand, using and within these constituent members, they unfold their essential being: first as group egos, and then as individual Egos.

6.2 The life kernels' unfolding of being through group egos

Guidance for the development of life kernels' essential being is carried out by higher powers through group egos or group souls. These group souls are lower beings, offspring or 'split-offs' from divine-spiritual beings. Group souls animate and direct the separate beings of the kingdoms of nature here on earth. The evolutionary impulses with which the primal beings are predisposed, come to expression in the working of the group souls, so that in a certain sense the primal beings themselves, in their still-dull consciousness, are also participating in this work. *Group souls direct consciously what is done and experienced by the primal beings more or less subconsciously*. So, as discussed above, human beings were already working on their physical body on Saturn despite still being united at that time in group souls. The primary group souls of the kingdoms of nature then subdivide into numerous sub-group souls.

Group souls of minerals are the offspring of the Thrones; those of plants, the offspring of the Spirits of Wisdom; those of animals, the Spirits of Movement; and those of man, the Spirits of Form. (GA 136, 13 April 1912, not quoted) These divine-spiritual beings are the higher group egos, so to speak, directing the lower group souls that derive from them. Referring to the group souls of animals, Rudolf Steiner says:

> [they] are, in a certain sense, lower images transformed—if we want to put it in terms of human language—into caricatures of the magnificent figures that permeate our cosmic consciousness beyond the spheres of the stars as the beings of the divine-spiritual hierarchies. . . . Don't take it in a derogatory sense when I say 'caricatures'. What from a humorous, artistic, human perspective is a caricature, is naturally something extraordinarily trivial when compared to the grandeur of caricature quality of the divine-spiritual beings in the world of the Moon sphere, which is also the world of group souls for the earthly animal kingdom. (GA 216, 16 September 1922)

Referring to animal instinct, which is an effect of the group soul, Steiner points to the higher group-soul quality of animals: 'Instinct is behaviour deriving from what—for example in my books *Theosophy* and *Occult Science*—is called spirit land.' (GA 237, 4 July 1924)

Some group souls take us back to very ancient times. Thus we find the statement that the group souls of plants, as offspring of the Spirits of Wisdom, 'have taken shape from the Spirits of Wisdom ever since the time when the Spirits of Wisdom themselves gave an etheric body to human beings out of their own substance'. (GA 136, 13 April 1912) This was during the Old Sun period when man's evolution was at the plant stage. These offspring, separated off from the Spirits of Wisdom during the Sun period, have thus also in subsequent periods remained the group souls of any beings at the plant stage. Following from this we can assume the mineral group souls were separated off from the Thrones already during the Saturn period, and have worked ever since as the group souls of each subsequent mineral kingdom. Animal group souls arose on Old Moon when man was at the animal stage; in the meantime they have become the group souls of the present animal kingdom. Group souls were directed on Saturn by the mineral group souls; on Old Sun, by plant group souls; on Old Moon, by animal group souls; and on earth they are subject to human group souls.

In the spiritual worlds there is no birth or death, only transformation. This also applies to group souls. 'This [animal] group soul certainly passes through youth, middle and old age, but its consciousness never ceases. It undergoes repeated transformations without passing through death; it transforms itself continually. Thus we can trace back an animal group soul into very, very ancient times; we only find metamorphosis, not birth and death.' (GA 101, 27 December 1907) 'When an animal species dies out, its group soul becomes that of another species. This, for the group soul, is something similar to a new birth.' (GA 98, 2 February 1908) When an animal species dies out, its etheric material remains behind. This must pass through the cosmos, then a new animal species can be formed from it. (GA 255, 20 July 1923, not quoted)

The group souls of minerals, plants, and animals live on the same cosmic planes as their elementary kingdoms. The chief group ego of the uniform mineral kingdom, as well as the sub-group egos of the various kinds of mineral, have their seat in the higher spirit region. They exert their influence from beyond the planetary system, raying in from all sides of cosmic space with differentiated qualities onto the minerals, making every mineral on earth the focus of these radial formations. The group egos of minerals have their astral body in the lower spirit region, and their etheric body on the astral plane. We find their physical body on the earth divided up into individual minerals.

The mineral group ego feels pleasure and pain. It feels pleasure when a mineral structure dissolves—for example, cooking salt in warm water. It feels pain when mineral substance solidifies, when salt dissolved in water precipitates out, by cooling, as solid salt crystals. 'Everything that today is solid, mineral, has crystallized out of the once-fluid earth. . . . For the sake of human existence it was necessary for the earth in its mineral being to pass through infinite pain; for, infinite pain was connected with this solidifying process of the earth.' (GA 105, 6 August 1908)

In the plant world 'there are all together seven group souls which, as plant souls, belong to the earth; all have their centre, in a certain sense, in the centre of the earth'. (GA 134, 1 January 1912) Elsewhere we find the statement that plant egos have their seat in the lower spirit region, which is represented by the sun; and it is from the sun that group egos of plants receive the impulses for their activity. 'But they are localized at the centre of the earth; it is there that all group egos of plants have their centre.' (GA 98, 15 January 1908) To understand this, we need to consider that the lower group egos of plants are united in the centre of the earth, whereas the hierarchical beings from which they arise, live in the sun. Since the various planetary spheres overlap, the centre of the earth coincides with that of the sun.

The plant world's astral body belongs to the astral body of the earth, it 'is the same as the earth's astral body itself, so the plant is thus immersed in the astral body of the earth.... From an occult point of view, we can regard the earth as a great organism, as a living being that has an astral body, and the various plants on our earth as members {of this astral body}. Each separate plant only has its own physical and etheric body.' (GA101, 26 December 1907) Because the astral body of the plant is the same as that of the earth, the consciousness of the plant world—not of individual plants—is also that of the earth, so that the consciousness of plant group egos is at the same time the consciousness of the earth. (GA 165, 31 December 1915, not quoted)

The earth, in its plant consciousness, experiences feelings of pleasure when individual plants are picked, for example by cows grazing on a meadow, or by the cutting of grass and corn; and pain when a plant is torn out by the roots.

The group egos of animals live on the astral plane, whereas each animal has its own astral and etheric body. (In lower animals, however, the astral body is not yet fully integrated into the physical.) The animal world was originally made up of seven principal groups. The highest group souls of these principal groups have their seat in the planets. Due to influences working in from forces of the zodiac, the seven principal groups specialized into the diversity we see in the animal world today. (GA 136, 13 April 1912, not quoted) Having as yet no Ego within it, the individual animal lives in dream pictures. Animal group egos have a wisdom greatly surpassing that of man, but they lack love. Only individual animals have love in the form of sexual and parental love, but this is instinctive. The death of an individual animal is, for the group ego, like the death of a limb which is then replaced by the birth of another animal.

The group egos of minerals, plants, and animals operate both in the higher beings of nature, and in man in the members of his being that belong to them. Accordingly, apart from the human Ego itself, there are other egos at work with their consciousness in the human structure.

> What forms the physical body is not under your control. Just as it is your Ego when you move your hand, so are you influenced by a higher world with regard to your physical body, with the ego-consciousness of the physical body which is the source of the body's physical processes. Only an initiate who can rise to the level of Intuition, gains power over his physical body so that no nerve stimulus passes along his nerves without him knowing it. Only then can he become a companion of those higher worlds that direct his physical body.... In the world of the harmony of the spheres, where the ego-consciousness of the plant world exists, is also the consciousness that permeates man's etheric body, living in him without his knowing it.... Just as the human being has an individual Ego, so there also lives in every astral body something of a group ego; this animal ego lives in the human astral body.... Only in his Ego does man have something into which no other being penetrates, no other consciousness-ego enters. (GA 99, 25 May 1907)

In the same way that the group ego of the animal kingdom is active in the human astral body, so is the plant kingdom in the human etheric body, and the mineral kingdom in the physical body.

The human kingdom itself originated from a common group ego. 'The way man received his group soul was such that, with the infusion of his Ego, a group soul was given as an outflow of the Spirits of Form.... Man was created as a unity over the earth, {a unity} through which the common primal Ego of man was to express itself as a group soul living in all human beings who had just descended to the physical plane.' (GA 136, 14 April 1912) The originally uniform primal Ego divided into four principal types which are symbolized in the image of the Lion, the Bull, the Eagle, and Man. Numerous intermediary stages then arose through the mixing of these four types. Human beings have developed themselves as more or less individual souls out of this group-soul situation.

Group souls and elementary kingdoms have the same origin, and unfold their activity from the same cosmic planes. Just as the group egos of minerals are the offspring of the Thrones, so also arising from the Thrones are the forces with which the first elementary kingdom shapes the physical forms of minerals. Likewise, the group egos of plants are the offspring of the same Spirits of Wisdom from whom the forces stem with which the second elementary kingdom structures the forms of plants. The Spirits of

Movement, whose offspring operate as the group egos of animals, also provided the forces with which the third elementary kingdom creates animal forms. The original group ego of human beings came from the Spirits of Form; they also offered up the forces with which man, as the fourth kingdom, forms his thoughts. And just as the first elementary kingdom unfolds its activity from the higher spirit region, the second from the lower spirit region, and the third from the astral plane, so the same applies to the corresponding group egos. The realms of forces that belong together work from the same cosmic planes. It is always the primal beings of the kingdoms of nature themselves which, using the forces with which they have been endowed, come to expression—although still without any independence or self-consciousness of their own—in the structuring and formation of their subtle bodies as well as in the unfolding of the nature of their essential being. They do this on the one hand as elemental beings, and on the other as group egos.

6.3 Working-together of elementary kingdoms and group egos

The elementary kingdoms and group egos must work together in order to enable the life kernels to develop in a harmonious way. Rudolf Steiner also lays stress on this collaboration.

> I have spoken to you previously about egos on the astral plane, the group egos of animals. Now we have another class of egos which live on the astral plane and exert an influence on people.... These are spirits that have never descended to the physical plane, spiritual beings who live on the astral plane and have a body of fire.... These beings of the third elementary kingdom are the companions of the animal group souls; they belong to the same region.... These egos work down from the astral plane as the animal group egos do in animals. Therefore we become aware of them as beings similar to animal group egos.... This is the third elementary kingdom; this kingdom shapes the drives and passions that are animal in nature.... Birds have very specific paths of migration. Who directs these migrations? The group souls of the birds. The instinct for the regular passage over the earth comes to expression in these migrations; this is directed by the species soul or group soul of the animal. On the other hand the animal's form, enabling it to have this instinct, to be a bearer of this instinct, is given by the beings of the third elementary kingdom, the companions of the animal group souls. Put somewhat trivially we could say: the egos which are the group souls of animals comprise *one* association on the astral plane; *another* association is formed by the beings of the third elementary kingdom.

But these must work together in peaceful harmony—the one giving the instincts, and the other the body for them, forming and shaping the body so that the instincts can come to expression.

Physical plant forms come from the beings of the second elementary kingdom. . . . The plant ego in the lower spirit region is a companion of the beings of the second elementary kingdom. And while the plant ego works on the plant from within, these beings work on it from without, form it, bring it to the point of opening and blossoming and so on. . . .

[The beings of the second elementary kingdom] have their ego in the lower spirit region. This ego has an even higher body {than that of the being on the astral plane with a body of fire} that has never even condensed to the point of warmth. . . . it has never entered the astral plane and has remained in the spirit region. . . . The second elementary kingdom works and shapes in a purer element; it shapes and articulates the forms of the plant. It also operates in man, in his many plant-like elements. . . . There is much in man that is of a vegetative nature, and in all this the beings of the second elementary kingdom exert an influence. So the forces of the second elementary kingdom are what constructs the body of the plant. In plants, the plant ego, which permeates the etheric and astral body*, and these beings of the second elementary kingdom work together. . . . The beings which work from the second elementary kingdom and cause the plants to shoot into form, fly in onto the plant from all sides like butterflies. They work on the repetition of leaf, flower, and so on. . . . The plant is a shaped plant due to the second elementary kingdom, otherwise it would be spherical. . . . In the mineral kingdom, apart from the mineral kingdom itself, there is also the first elementary kingdom; hence we have a shaped mineral kingdom. . . . The forces of the mineral, which operate as repulsion and attraction, atomic forces, stem from the group souls of the minerals. The beings of the first elementary kingdom are what give minerals their form. . . . The formative forces of minerals, which work out of a sphere of formlessness, are to be found in the higher spirit region. . . .

These other egos have gradually remained behind the human kingdom. They constitute the hidden realms, the elemental realms that lie behind our physical world and send their influences into it. . . . The three elementary kingdoms interpenetrate, flow into one another. We will never come to real concepts if we imagine everything in separate

* Footnote: It is not clear in which sense Steiner means 'astral body' here, since the plant's astral body is really the ambient astrality of the whole earth.

> boxes. . . . Our world is something with many intersections; only when we make our concepts fluid do we gradually reach a comprehension of things. . . . From this we can see that getting anywhere in spiritual science requires patience. Anyone wishing to understand the divine must have endless patience, for the divine encompasses *everything*. (GA 98, 4 December 1907)

Thus it is always the form that is shaped by the formative forces of the elementary kingdoms, and by means of this that the group egos can unfold their activity. The elemental-kingdom beings are also ego beings in so far as they are the life kernels of the nature kingdoms, cloaked in the thought-seed substance of the higher spirit region. But they are still dependent ego beings without any consciousness of their own.

The elementary kingdoms work on earth's creatures from without. Hence it is said of the beings of the second elementary kingdom that they 'fly in onto the plant from all sides like butterflies'. This applies also to the plant forces working in man. It is in this sense that we can understand what, in Scene VIII of the Mystery Drama *The Souls' Awakening*, is beheld by the neophyte while outside his physical body during the act of initiation: the weaving and working of the beings of the second elementary kingdom on the physical body's organs of life.

Scene 8: {literal translation}

> . . . I saw how my living earthly form
> was held outside myself like another being.
> . . . .
> The light of spirits of higher worlds streamed towards it—
> Beings approached it like butterflies, bright and shimmering,
> who actively took care of its life.
> My body reflected back a sparkling play of colour
> from the flickering light of these beings,
> which showed itself glittering nearby, glimmering at a distance,
> finally scattering and losing itself in space.
> . . . .
> (GA 14, *The Souls' Awakening*)

6.4 The elementary kingdoms and the states of matter

The further our solar system advanced in its development, the more complicated became the connections between the active powers and forces within it. 'With each new embodiment—that is, the Saturn, Sun, Moon, and earth conditions—there was a different way of collaborating amongst these hierarchical beings because each condition through which our earth has passed presented a particular task these hierarchies had set for themselves.' (GA 121, 11 June 1910)

Warmth is the outer expression of elemental-etheric beings which in spiritual science are called elemental beings or etheric formative forces. Thus the warmth of Saturn arose by the Thrones 'exuding' lower, serving beings of this nature from their own substance. And the Thrones' condensing of Saturn warmth was a process of transforming part of this warmth into beings of the aeriform, watery and solid states, enchanting them, as it were, into these forms of substance.

> When warmth becomes so strong that it begins to glow and make smoke, then something of the spiritual element that was in the warmth has to enter the smoke. And this spiritual element that was in the warmth, that makes a transition into smoke, into an aeriform state, is now spellbound in the smoke, in that which appears as a darkening. Spiritual beings that are with the smoke have to put up, so to speak, with being enchanted into becoming denser, into becoming smoke.... Spiritual beings, which we also call elemental beings, are spellbound in all air; and they become even more spellbound, exiled to a still lower form of existence so to speak, when air is converted to water. Therefore, in everything that is externally perceptible, spiritual science sees something that has its origin in this primal condition of fire or warmth, and then first became air or smoke or gas by the warmth condensing to gas, then the gas to fluid, the fluid to solid.... So, fundamentally, we have nothing but fire. Everything is fire, but condensed fire: gold, silver, copper are condensed fire. Everything was once fire, everything was born from fire; but in all this condensed state there is a spiritual element that lies spellbound within it.... And we look around us and say: these beings, whom we thank for everything around us, had to descend out of the element of fire and are held enchanted in all things. (GA 110, 12 April 1909, evening)

Thus the beings which as elemental beings bring about the sense-perceptible phenomena of earth existence, all arose as fire beings out of substance of the Thrones' own being; and they continue to work today out of this Throne-substance from which they originate.

The Thrones remained closely connected with the elemental-physical substances that they themselves were condensing out of warmth; thus in the Sun period {they were connected} with the aeriform element; in the Moon period, with the watery element; and in the earth period, with the solid element. On the other hand, governance over the substance-forces was gradually transferred to the beings of the second hierarchy as the Thrones relinquished it by aligning themselves with the substances in the process of condensing. Thus during the Sun period the governance over warmth was taken on by the Spirits of Wisdom (Kyriotetes); in the Moon period, by the Spirits of Movement (Dynamis); and in the earth era, by the Spirits of Form (Exusiai). The being-substance of the Thrones still continues to work in today's warmth, but governed and managed by the Spirits of Form. The relation of the second-hierarchy beings to the airy and watery elements changed in the same way, as the following table shows:

Embodiments of the earth	Governing beings over the elemental-physical forces of substance			
	Warmth	***Air***	***Water***	***Solid***
Saturn	Thrones			
Sun	Kyriotetes	Thrones		
Moon	Dynamis	Kyriotetes	Thrones	
earth	Exusiai	Dynamis	Kyriotetes	Thrones

With regard to the present-day relation of the higher powers to the elemental-physical forces of substance that are the active forces behind mineral-physical substance, we read:

> Thus behind the solid ground beneath us we see the Spirits of Will, and behind, not the physical water, but the forces which constitute the fluid element, we have the activity of the Spirits of Wisdom. . . . In so far as it is caused by forces hidden behind it, we can regard the aeriform element that weaves and holds sway in our surroundings as the outflow of activity . . . of the Spirits of Movement. . . . And when we penetrate through to the warmth element, it is the Spirits of Form that live and weave there. . . . The very fact that [the outspread solid element] brings to manifestation the likes of what we call material existence, tells us that it has the being-nature of the Thrones. The fact that it has taken on shape, that this primal substance, as it were, is always shaped into forms, reveals that it is the outer manifestation of the Elohim. . . . They are active there, the smiths in their warmth element, and smithy out of the formless substance of the Spirits of Will the crystalline forms of the various rock types and metals. . . . Behind what our senses see around us lies an elemental existence, an earthy element; but in truth Spirits of Will live in this earthy element. Behind this is a fluid element; but in this live in truth Spirits of Wisdom. Behind this is an airy element; but in this live in truth Spirits of Movement. And a warmth element in

> which in truth live Spirits of Form, the Elohim. But we mustn't think that we can keep these spheres strictly apart, that we can fix firm boundaries between them. Our whole earthly life rests on the fact that the watery, airy, and solid elements work into one another, that warmth penetrates and permeates everything.... We find warmth everywhere in the other elemental stages of existence. We may say therefore that we find the working of the Elohim—the actual force element in warmth—absolutely everywhere, ... this element of warmth that is the manifestation of the Spirits of Form. (GA 122, 22 August 1910)

The Spirits of Form reveal themselves in light. 'Wherever something lights up, we have in the light the garment of high beings, ... of Spirits of Form.' (GA105, 7 August 1908) The actual force element through which the Spirits of Form operate however, is warmth—Throne-substance that has remained at the Saturn stage.

The relation of the hierarchical beings to *etheric forces* has remained unchanged. Still today behind warmth-ether lies the substance of Throne-being; behind light-ether, that of Spirits of Wisdom; behind chemical ether, that of the Spirits of Movement; and life-ether, the Spirits of Form. Higher ethers retain the forces of the lower ones. 'The present relation of etheric forces to one another is such that the later, more highly developed ether always contains the attributes of the earlier, despite, as a new entity, developing a completely different quality of activity.' (Guenther Wachsmuth, *Die ätherischen Bildekräfte in Kosmos, Erde und Mensch* (Etheric formative forces in cosmos, earth and man)), Chap 2)

The other ethers are thus contained in the life-ether streaming to us from the sun. Only as they draw close to earth's periphery do they each separate out of the life-ether into the ether zones encompassing the earth. The following statements of Rudolf Steiner can be understood bearing this in mind.

> Light is the element in which the Spirits of Form initially live and weave. But it is due to the action of light and everything it contains that solid forms are created. Initially man has no organs that can enable him to see what lies behind those forces of light—which we also call the Spirits of Form—no organs enabling him to see what is woven into the light. Everything on our earth which causes decomposition and synthesis, everything acting as chemical forces, is still woven here into the light, and this is essentially the terrain in which the Spirits of Movement are active. When we learn to perceive something in the reactions of chemical decomposition and synthesis—which we usually

see only as *maya*—then we hear these Spirits of Movement, then we perceive the music of the spheres spoken of by the Pythagorean and other mystery schools.... Then there are also the Spirits of Wisdom who send in their influences from outside, and who work into the weaving light and the music of the spheres weaving through space. Such is the life of the cosmic ethers raying onto the earth. Life streams from cosmic space to the earth and is 'captured' by earth's beings. This comes from the Spirits of Wisdom. Thus we gaze into cosmic distances and look up first to the sun in which these forces are concentrated for us, and see how out of space comes streaming Life, weaving Tone, forming Light—the threefoldness of the second hierarchy. (GA 121, 11 June 1910)

There is therefore also warmth-ether in sunlight; Throne-substance is at work in it. And the life of cosmic ether raying onto the earth from the sun is the light-ether of the Spirits of Wisdom. Thus the Spirits of Form work through life-ether, generating solid forms; the Spirits of Movement in sound- or chemical-ether; the Spirits of Wisdom in light-ether; and the Thrones in warmth-ether. This means that the hierarchical beings working through etheric forces are not the same as those working through the elemental-physical forces of substance. This gives us the following picture for present earth existence:

Acting Hierarchical Beings

in the elemental-physical forces of substance		**in the ethers**	
Warmth	Exusiai	**Warmth-ether**	Thrones
Air	Dynamis	**Light-ether**	Kyriotetes
Water	Kyriotetes	**Chemical-ether**	Dynamis
Solid	Thrones	**Life-ether**	Exusiai

These opposite sequences of hierarchical beings can possibly be clarified by the fact that increasingly stronger forces are needed to manage the denser states of substance than is the case for the increasingly more rarefied etheric forces. This is why the sequence of states of substance begins with the Spirits of Form and finishes with the higher—and therefore more powerful—Thrones. By contrast the denser warmth-ether is governed by the Thrones, and the finer life-ether by the Spirits of Form.

Connected with this change in the hierarchical beings' relation to the elemental-physical forces of substance, is a corresponding change in their relation to the etheric forces. Although the elementary kingdoms continue to work out of the same being-substance of the hierarchies from which they received their original attributes—the first elementary kingdom from the being-substance of the Thrones; the second, from the Spirits of Wisdom; the third, from the Spirits of Movement; and the fourth, from the Spirits of Form—the assignment of the elementary kingdoms to substances and etheric forces has changed. Thus the first elementary kingdom no longer operates through warmth-ether in warmth (as was the case on Old Saturn), but works through life-ether on what is solid; the second kingdom no longer operates through light-ether in the airy element (as on Old Sun), but works through chemical-ether on what is fluid; the third kingdom no longer operates through chemical-ether on the watery element (as on Old Moon), but through light-ether on what is aeriform; and the fourth kingdom operates through warmth-ether in the warmth-element.

We need to add that, just like substances and etheric forces, the elementary kingdoms also interpenetrate one another. 'The three elementary kingdoms interpenetrate, flow into one another ... if we imagine everything in separate boxes we will never reach a true idea of it.... Our world is something with many intersections; we will be able gradually to apprehend the matter only if we keep our concepts fluid.' (GA 98, 4 December 1907)

The first elementary kingdom is the formative agency in everything at the physical level: in other words, in the warmth, aeriform, fluid, and solid elements. Only the solid element, however, is formed by first-kingdom forces working on their own; the other states of substance are worked upon by the other elementary kingdoms as well, together with the first. For only solid things are subject to earthly laws; the other states of substance are influenced additionally by super-physical forces working in from worlds beyond the earth. In ancient Greece:

> [they called] what is solid, 'earth', because they wished to express thereby that when a body solidifies it comes completely under the influence of terrestrial laws. On the other hand, when a body becomes 'water' it is no longer under the influence of purely earthly laws but under the influence of the entire planetary system. The governing forces in a fluid body, in 'water', do not stem only from the earth but from the planetary system.
>
> They felt, when they called solid bodies 'earth', that only these were subject to terrestrial laws, and that when a body melted it came under laws that were extraterrestrial. And when they called an aeriform body 'air', they had the feeling that such a body was under the influence of

the unifying being of the sun. And they perceived the nature of earthly air as given essentially—in its configuration, its inner constitution and substantiality—by the active forces of the sun.... The solidification of bodies was only possible because the earth emancipated itself, so to speak, from the cosmos, pulled itself free, gave itself independent laws, whereas the aeriform element 'air', for example, remains subject in its laws to the influences of the sun-being that are unified for the whole earth. (GA 321, 2 March 1920)

The streams of life—that is, the etheric forces—belonging to the mineral element come essentially from the planets, whereas the astral element streams to this minerality from the sun. (GA 136, 14 April 1912, not quoted) This means that in the fluid element, apart from physical forces, there are also etheric forces at work, and in the air element also astral forces. At another time Rudolf Steiner also indicated that only dead earthly matter is governed purely by terrestrial laws. 'If we penetrate into the element of water, we experience the world itself as a great living being, for we are carried out into the cosmos with its wellsprings of life; we experience the world as something alive. When we come into the rhythmic element [air], we experience the world as suffused through and through with soul. And if we then penetrate into the warmth-element, we experience the world as permeated through and through by spirit.' (GA 205, 28 June 1921) Thus in the human physical body for example, which is composed of a solid, a fluid, a gaseous, and a warmth organism, only the solid organism is governed by physical forces. In the fluid organism, which lies behind our life of ideation, the etheric body is at work through chemical-ether. The aeriform organism, the bearer of our life of feeling, is energized by the astral body through light-ether. And in the warmth organism, the Ego energizes its will impulses through warmth-ether. (GA 202, 17 December 1920, not quoted)

Accordingly, in the watery element there are not only the physical forces of the first elementary kingdom at work through life-ether, but also the etheric forces of the second kingdom through chemical-ether, which give 'water' its characteristic qualities. In the airy element, the active forces of the first and second elementary kingdoms gain the addition of the astral forces of the third kingdom through light-ether, which bring air as such to manifestation. And in warmth the spiritual forces of the fourth kingdom also come into play through warmth-ether. Thus a substance's form of manifestation is determined by the highest elementary kingdom at work within it; the activity of the other kingdoms withdraws into the background but is nevertheless still present. For if the airy and watery elements did not contain the physical forces of life-ether, they would disperse into space. They too are subject to earthly laws, albeit in diluted form.

7. Substances in the subtle 'garments' of the life kernel

7.1 The primordial substance and its forms of densification

In lectures where his starting point is the Sankhya philosophy of ancient India, Rudolf Steiner describes the substances in which spirit-beings as life kernels envelop themselves, and out of which, in lower worlds, they form their subtle bodies. This philosophy assumed a primordial substance {or *prima materia*} from which all other conditions of substance condensed. This highest form of substance is the same as that of which spirit-man consists.

> What will one day be a subtle garment (*Hülle*) of the human being, in which the soul-spiritual core of man, spirit-man, will clothe itself as it were—this will indeed have a significance for people only in the future. But in the great universe what a being's development is evolving towards always already exists.... The substance is therefore already there in the universe of which human spirit-man will one day consist.... And what exists in this way in the universe, not yet individualized but like undifferentiated spiritual waters filling space and time, what thus existed, and will exist, and from which all formations emerge—this was called the highest form of substance by Sankhya philosophy. It is the form of substance that is assumed in Sankhya philosophy from eternity to eternity.... Just as we speak of everything at the beginning of earth evolution, of everything that was still to become earth evolution, as existing in spirit, as substance of spirit-being, so Sankhya philosophy spoke of its primal substance, of its primordial ocean, so to speak, from which all other forms, physical and super-physical, then evolved. (GA 142, 29 December 1912)

Sankhya philosophy called this *prima materia* in its various forms of manifestation *prakriti*, and the soul-spiritual element which clothed itself in this substance it called *purusha*.

> In forms, or in prakriti which encompasses all forms from the dense physical body right up to the primordial ocean, in this prakriti lives purusha, the soul-spiritual element which was thought of as monads in separate souls. Thus the separate soul-monads were seen as being equally without beginning or end as this material principle of prakriti—not 'material' in our materialistic sense, but imagined as without beginning or end. This philosophy thus conceived of a pluralism of

> souls that submerse themselves in the prakriti principle and evolve downwards from the highest and undifferentiated form of the primal waters with which they enveloped themselves, to the point of embodiment in a dense physical body. Then they begin the return: having overcome the dense physical body, they develop themselves back to the primordial ocean, only to free themselves also from this, and enter purusha as a free soul. (GA 142, 29 December 1912)

In Sankhya philosophy 'the individual soul was seen as something real that is entangled and linked to fundamental materiality, taking on the most varied forms within this basic material, and thereby manifesting externally in different forms. A soul clothes itself with the basic material element, which, like the soul, is seen as being eternal.' (GA 142, 28 December 1912) The term 'material' is therefore not to be understood here in the sense of physical matter but as the highly spiritual, primal substance which is able to condense itself by degrees to the point of physical matter, and thus lies behind all phenomena in the world—spiritual, soul-astral, and physical.

Later in the lectures referred to above, we find the following concerning this gradual densification of primal substance:

> So to begin with we have the most aboriginal form, so to speak, of this material element as a kind of primordial spiritual ocean into which the soul submerses itself. If we were to turn our gaze to the beginning stages of evolution, we would find the material element in an undifferentiated state as it were, and a plurality of souls diving down into it in order to undergo further stages of evolution. The first form that we find at the very beginning of evolution therefore, is spiritual substance itself, but not yet differentiated out from the uniform quality of the primal ocean.
>
> The next thing to emerge, with which the soul can now clothe itself individually, is buddhi. So when we think of a soul clothed in primordial-ocean substance, this state of being does not yet distinguish the soul from the general swell of the primal waters. By clothing itself not only in this first existence of primal waters, but also in what emerges subsequently, the soul can clothe itself in buddhi.
>
> The third element that emerges, and through which the souls can become more and more individual, is ahamkara. These are all lower and lower formations of the primal material. So we have the primal material, then its subsequent form—buddhi—and following this, ahamkara. The next form is manas, followed by sense organs, followed in turn by the more rarefied elements {ethers}, and finally the material elements we find in our physical environment. (GA 142, 28 December 1912)

> Whereas buddhi is only at the border, so to speak, of the differentiation principle, only hints at a certain individualization, ahamkara {on the other hand} emerges in completely differentiated form; so when we speak of ahamkara we need to imagine that buddhi organizes itself downwards to the point of independent, existential, substantial forms which thus exist individually in the world. In order to get a picture of this evolution, we need to imagine a uniform mass of water as the substance of the primal principle; this then wells up so that shapes that do not yet break free as complete droplets begin to form, shapes that rise up like little water mounds from the general substance, but whose base is in the common primal waters—here we have buddhi. And as these water mounds break free as droplets, as independent spheres, there we have the form of ahamkara. Through a certain condensing of this ahamkara—the already individualized form of each separate soul—there emerges what we call manas. (GA 142, 29 December 1912)

The fact that the various conditions of substance that shape themselves from the primal waters are referred to by Rudolf Steiner as 'forms', indicates that these conditions mean the same as what in spiritual science is called the Conditions of Form or Stages of Form. It is the passage of souls through the Stages of Form discussed above. Beings build their subtle bodies out of the primal ocean and its forms of densification.

In modern spiritual science the Sankhya concepts of ahamkara and manas are combined in the concept of spirit-self. Ahamkara 'is the principle behind the human individuality which causes ... the human being to feel himself as a separate being.' Ahamkara, according to the ancient Indian view, appears in 'independent, existential, substantial forms which thus exist individually in the world'. Corresponding with this, we find in *Theosophy* the following with reference to spirit-self:

> What [man] truly is as a spirit in spirit land only becomes apparent when he ascends during the intermediary state between two incarnations into the fifth region of spirit land. What he is here is truly himself. It is that which in numerous incarnations receives an external existence.... We see that what in this book is called *spirit-self*, lives in this region, according to its stage of development, in the reality appropriate to it. (GA 9, *The Three Worlds IV*)

But, indeed, only 'according to its stage of development'. This means that the form of spirit-self, as well as that of life-spirit and spirit-man, are to be understood for the time being in an ideal sense. These highest members of man's being are his only in a germinal state, still waiting to be developed.

Manas—which corresponds in spiritual science to spirit-self—is the term used by Sankhya philosophy for 'the inner sense' which, as 'a generalized, comprehensive sense, does not extend over separate areas of sense but lives in our inner being and fills us as though with a single sensing as we inwardly work on separate sense-impressions'. The separate senses differentiate out from this general sense, and the various sense-impressions integrate themselves in it into a whole.

> Manas differentiates separate forms, it provides the supersensory forces that constitute our individual senses.... The soul is connected with the outer world through the energies of the senses.... Seen as a sum of forces, we summarize this energetic connectedness as the astral body. From these sense forces that differentiated out from manas, there arise in turn the finer elements which we think of as constituting the etheric body. (GA 142, 29 December 1912)

Then the final phase of densification is the physical body.

> Thus Sankhya philosophy gives us a complete presentation, so to speak, of the human constitution and how the human being in the past, present and future, clothes itself as a soul in the substantiality of the external nature principle, whereby under 'nature' we must understand not only its external, visible aspects, but all levels of nature right up to the most invisible. (GA 142, 29 December 1912)

If we combine the ahamkara and manas of Sankhya philosophy into spirit-self, we get six stages of form. According to modern spiritual science, however, the Ego must be added, which was not yet a consideration in those ancient times. The Ego-structure belongs to the fourth region of spirit land, spirit-self to the fifth, life-spirit to the sixth, and spirit-man to the seventh. Taken together with the astral, etheric and physical bodies in the lower worlds, this again gives us seven stages of form.

Thus at the beginning of a world evolution we have a mysterious, undifferentiated primal substance which we are to imagine as eternal, without beginning or end, out of which condensed, so to speak, all the forms of substance in the three worlds from the finest spiritual to the densest material conditions, and into which they then dissolve again.

The primal substance of Sankhya philosophy lying behind all conditions of substance in the three worlds is evidently the same as what Rudolf Steiner calls the 'neutral cosmic fire' existing at the beginning of our cycle of creation, into which the Thrones pour the substance of their being. So, in the description of the emergence of ancient Saturn, we read: 'Now initially it is the Thrones who exert their influence on this fire formation that we call Old Saturn.... They trickle their warmth substance, so to speak, into this Saturnian mass.' (GA 110, 17 April 1909) But this suggests that a 'Saturnian mass' was already there when the Thrones began to pour their own substance into this fire formation of Saturn. And Rudolf Steiner then continues:

> Now we can ask: what is the situation with this substance? Was a warmth substance already there beforehand? What was there already we can really only call a kind of neutral cosmic fire that is basically one and the same as cosmic space; so I could just as well say that beforehand only space was present, as though with a boundary, and that now into the surface there was trickled what we can call the warmth substance of ancient Saturn. (GA 110, 17 April 1909)

In other words, before the actual beginning of Saturn's development there was already a type of cosmic fire which did not just fill out space but with its substance actually constituted it. This cosmic fire was still completely 'neutral', did not yet hold any creative or formative impulses, rested in itself, so to speak, in a completely undetermined state. Of course 'space' should not be understood here in the present three-dimensional sense of the word. Also, Steiner does not say that space is there 'with a boundary', but 'as though with a boundary', thereby trying to symbolize the purely spiritual process. Equally we should not imagine the neutral cosmic fire that was one with cosmic space, nor the warmth substance with which the Thrones worked into it, as being sense-perceptible in any form. All these events at the beginning of Old Saturn's development took place initially on the arupa plane, in the world of still-formless thought-seeds, where the thoughts of the gods do not yet have any defined form but are contemplated by them for the time being only as intentions, as aims. The gods were still meditating, we could say, on what they intended to formulate further and think out in clear images in the future. Only in the further course of Saturn's development did the contemplation of the gods condense to thought-forms, to archetypes, from which formations as images of the archetypes could arise in the lower worlds.

Only by the Thrones, with support from the Cherubim and Seraphim, pouring the fire of their will into the *prima materia*—the original cosmic fire that was already there but still neutral—did this primal substance first become actual Saturn-warmth substance. 'We see how the first stage of the gods' plans is realized in the flowing down of fire-substance from the Thrones, by the Thrones pouring their own substance, the substance of the original cosmic fire, into the space which had been allocated so to speak for a new cosmic system. . . . From their own being the Thrones pour primal fire into this sphere of space.' (GA 110, 14 April 1909)

What in *these* words is called the 'original cosmic fire' and 'primal fire' poured by the Thrones into the 'space' as 'their' sacrificial substance, is no longer *neutral* cosmic fire, no longer the primal substance in its original state—which is what the Saturnian mass had consisted of before the intervention of the Thrones—but is that original cosmic fire out of which the Thrones had shaped their physical body in earlier ages, subsequently transforming it into spirit-man and thereby spiritualizing it to the highest form of primal substance. Thus it is primal substance permeated by the fire of Throne-will. This 'primal fire' flowing out from the Thrones must have been of a different nature from the original, neutral, cosmic fire because, through the inflow of fire substance from the Thrones, the neutral fire changed within the Saturnian mass into something different: namely, into Saturn's actual warmth-substance. Rudolf Steiner also speaks later of a threefold fire being involved in the creation of Saturn: of fire working in from outside (the Thrones), of an inner fire (generated by other divine-spiritual beings as their forces worked into the interior of Saturn), and a neutral fire (the original Saturnian mass). These other beings were the members of the second hierarchy who were at work in the surroundings of Saturn. 'Just as our earth is enveloped by an atmosphere, so too was Saturn; on Saturn, however, this atmosphere was of a spiritual nature.' (GA 110, 13 April 1909, morning)

> As soon as this warmth-substance [of the Thrones] was poured drop by drop into Old Saturn, the beings that come into question on both sides were also active. Here in the interior of the Saturnian space we find the Spirits of Form, the Spirits of Movement, and the Spirits of Wisdom; they are active in the interior. Working inwards from outside are Cherubim, Seraphim and Thrones. And the result is that a collaboration takes place between the beings outside and the beings within. We saw that we can distinguish inner soul fire which is felt as a comfort of inner warmth, and fire that is outwardly perceptible. In the middle between these two is neutral warmth. This neutral warmth is actually here in this egg-form [of Saturn]. By contrast we find soul warmth spread out over all this, as though radiating in from outside, but holding back. It is as though soul warmth radiated in from outside but then held back from the neutral fire there inside. The warmth that is actually perceptible is repelled from the interior. So we actually have [Saturn] enclosed by two streams: an outer stream of soul warmth, and an inner

> stream of soul warmth which would be perceptible for an external sense. In other words, only what is in the interior is physically perceptible warmth. (GA 110, 17 April 1909)

By the Thrones working into the surface of Saturn with their fiery will, they enabled the beings of the second hierarchy to generate inner warmth in the neutral cosmic fire in Saturn's interior, which then gradually converted into outer warmth. 'That is the strange thing about evolution on Saturn: warmth gradually converts, so to speak, from being purely inward at the beginning of Saturn to being outwardly perceptible at the end.' (GA 110, 13 April 1909, morning) This outwardly or physically perceptible warmth, however, would only have been perceptible to clairvoyant vision, for it was physical warmth in an elemental form of existence. As discussed in Chapter 5, Saturn warmth was a simultaneous interweaving of both etheric and physical warmth. And because warmth-ether is attributed in spiritual science to the physical plane, Rudolf Steiner could call Saturn both a 'rarefied, subtle, etheric' warmth body, and a 'physical' one. As a physical body Saturn could not be permeated by the soul warmth of the Thrones. This is why the fire of Throne-will flowed only up to the surface of Saturn, 'only up to its limit, so to speak', without penetrating it; it thus enveloped it only from outside.

The densification of the primal substance began with the processes described in broad terms above, whereby the originally neutral cosmic fire was transformed, by the inflow of substance from the Thrones' own being, into the thought-seed substance of the physical level, and then into the warmth-substance of Saturn from which all subsequent forms of substance in our cycle of creation arose.

7.2 *Substances as living beings*

To the question as to what the substances of the spiritual, astral, etheric and physical levels are in themselves, Rudolf Steiner gives an answer that is as unambiguous as it is difficult for human minds to comprehend: they are *beings* of the most diverse kinds imaginable. For, fundamentally, there is:

> nothing in the universe other than consciousnesses. Anything beyond the consciousness of any kind of being belongs to the sphere of *maya* or the great illusion.... So we can really only describe consciousnesses when we describe realities..... The realities of the world are beings in different conditions of consciousness. The fact that we live at the human level of consciousness, and due to this consciousness do not have a full perspective over the realities, has the effect that what has no reality appears to us as having reality. (GA 148, 18 December 1913)

> Seen from the spiritual world, the attributes, forces, and substances of the sense-world disappear; they reveal themselves as mere appearances. And what one has left of this world is beings. True reality lies in these beings. The case is similar with the elemental world. Here too, when looking from the perspective of the spiritual world, everything that is not a being disappears.... The supersensory world reveals itself finally as a world of beings and of what still remains of these beings externally as the expression of their deeds. But the sense and elemental worlds manifest as the deeds of spiritual beings as well. (GA 17, 'Cosmic spiritual beings')

'Everything that happens materially is indeed only the expression of spiritual facts, and all things that we find at the material level are only the external "casing" of spiritual beings.... Everything that happens is caused by multitudes of higher and lower spiritual beings of the spiritual hierarchies.' (GA 110, 12 April 1909) In the astral or soul world 'the distinction between "energy" {or "force"}and "matter" cannot be as clear-cut as it is in the physical world. An instinct can just as well be called "energy" as "matter".' (GA 9, *The Three Worlds*) Energy is always the manifestation of the activity of a being. For example, what we call a blow is an expression of energy, 'is something which a living being, when it strikes another, carries out from deep within the living being itself'. (GA 117, 4 December 1909) Hence everything appearing as substance, whether sense-perceptible or supersensory, is nothing other than the revelation of beings or their activity. We need to make a distinction here between the hierarchical beings themselves and lower, non-independent beings through which the hierarchies operate in the earth's processes of nature. For, at the present time, the gods themselves are active only in the soul-spiritual aspect of man. In all the processes of nature on the other hand they employ certain lower beings which they have 'secreted' out of themselves, and through which they manifest and realize their thoughts from the past. They also work through lower beings of this kind in the processes in man that belong to nature.

Luciferic and ahrimanic beings also have lower beings of this kind that they have exuded from themselves. Thus, with reference to retarded Spirits of Movement who operate like Spirits of Form, we find the following: 'These spirits, each of which in turn has many below it—because each one generates many spiritually lower-level beings—are enveloped in the spiritual world by a quantity of spiritual beings which are always subordinate to the hierarchies in question.... These abnormal Spirits of Form ... have their own subordinate spirits as well.' (GA 121, 11 June 1910)

Such 'secretions' of the most varied kinds are to be found in connection with all the higher hierarchies. The first and second hierarchies manifest their own being through them, objectivize themselves as it were in their 'secretions', which then remain as beings much as a snail secretes out of itself its shell.

> What the beings of the second hierarchy objectivize, what they create out of themselves, endures for as long as they remain connected with what they have created. These beings of the second hierarchy can create something like an image of themselves; this, however, remains connected with them, and cannot separate from them; it remains in a certain way connected to them.... What they create would be dead and disintegrate if they themselves did not remain connected with it. (GA 136, 7 April 1912)

The manifestations of these hierarchical beings are always associated with the quickening of life.

> With regard to the beings of the first hierarchy, the situation is that they also objectivize themselves, they press out their own being, separate it off as though in a skin, in a shell, which however is the expression of their own being. This now sloughs off from them and remains in the world, even when they separate from it.... The life in the beings of the first hierarchy is such that it perceives itself by giving rise to objective, independent beings of this kind that separate off. The inner condition of consciousness for the beings of the first hierarchy, their inner experience, lies in creating, in making beings independent.... Creating worlds is their outer life, creating beings is their inner life. (GA 136, 7 April 1912)

Rudolf Steiner calls the Spirits of Cycles of Time, and other beings at work in nature, the offspring of the beings of the first hierarchy. The offspring of the second hierarchy are the beings which as group-souls 'permeate and quicken the beings of the kingdoms of nature'. (GA 136, 6 April 1912) Etheric beings too are the offspring of the second hierarchy and of the Thrones, from whom etheric forces originate. The offspring of the third hierarchy are the elemental beings working at the physical level.

The spiritual bodily nature of the independent higher beings is formed by non-independent lower beings; through these {lower} beings they reveal themselves and operate in the processes of the world. 'These beings of the higher hierarchies do not have earthly or physical substance in what we would call their bodily nature: they have spiritual substance.' (GA 230, 21 October 1923) At the end of his final address, Rudolf Steiner referred to certain 'bright ether-beings' who form the garment of the time-spirit Michael:

> Springing from Powers of the Sun,
> Radiant Spirit-powers, blessing all Worlds!
> For Micha-el's garment of rays
> Ye are predestinèd by Thought Divine.
> (GA 238, 28 September 1924,
> translation by George and Mary Adams)

In the battle against the ahrimanic dragon, Michael assists man through the fact that 'in the human being there lives an etheric image of Michael, and this wages the actual battle in man'. (GA 223, 27 September 1923) We should also think of this etheric image of Michael as a being that has separated off from him.

The offspring of beings of the first hierarchy, the *Spirits of Cycles of Time*, who belong to the astral body of the earth, could be called the 'commanders' of the elemental beings. Rudolf Steiner calls them a 'multiplicity, a plurality, a swelling sea of spirits', without going into details about their various kinds. However, since they stem from the three different groups of beings in the first hierarchy, they must themselves differ in nature. These 'Spirits of Cycles of Time, which are spread around the whole earth, present what we could call the earth's astral body.... This astral body is connected with the earth and consists of higher spirits ... which surround the earth planet and permeate it like a spiritual atmosphere.' (GA 136, 4 April 1912)

The Spirits of Cycles of Time have the task, as 'commanders' as it were of the nature spirits, to lead their work and administer it over the seasons of the year.

> All kinds of arrangements in time, of administering relationships in time and space, are connected with these beings.... So not only the regular course of the year in the growth and dying away of plants, but also the regular cycle that comes to expression on the earth in day and night, is caused by beings of this kind which are to be reckoned as belonging to the astral body of the earth. Everything that is connected with rhythmic repetitions, rhythmic alternation, with changes in time and time relationships that re-occur—all this is ordered by these spiritual beings.

The spinning of the earth about its own axis also occurs because 'around the whole earth are spread out the Spirits of Cycles of Time who are the real bearers of the forces that turn the earth about its axis. It is extraordinarily important that we see in the astral body of the earth everything that is connected with regular change, with the blooming and fading of plants, but also everything connected with the alternation of day and night, in the seasons, in the times of the day and so on. (GA 136, 4 April 1912) The Spirits of Cycles of Time also order 'those rhythmic periodicities whereby, for example, the members of a particular animal species have a specific length of life in which they develop from birth to death'. (GA 136, 7 April 1912)

The guidance of nature spirits by the Spirits of Cycles of Time goes into fine detail. Thus, at a certain time of the year, for example,

> certain Spirits of the Cycles of Time [combine] the influences in the plant of the forces of movement coming from the planets and which have a spiral-causing effect, and the forces coming from the sun.... When the growth cycle of the plant is complete—that is, when the Spirits of the Cycles of Time combine the activity of planetary spirits with the activity of the sun spirit—then the parts of the now-complete plant which had hitherto followed the planets in a spiral pattern, now order themselves neatly into a circle around the stamens, and stem growth comes to completion in the ovaries—these two are combined together. Plant growth is completed by the activity of the Spirits of Cycles of Time joining the activities of the Spirits of Movement and the Spirits of Wisdom, or of their off-spring. (GA 136, 13 April 1912)

It appears that the following indication is also referring to the working of the Spirits of Cycles of Time. The seer can see how the spiritual worlds:

> spread out an elemental realm about us here on earth that is the foundation of the realm of nature, and that certain forces stream down so that these {elemental} beings receive the power at springtime to shape and bring forth out of the earth its covering of plants. Certain spirit beings bring down the forces of the Spirits of Form, imparting them to elemental beings so that a new world of form shoots forth at springtime. And thus an interplay takes place in the course of the year between the spirits of the higher hierarchies and the elemental beings that live and weave in nature that surrounds us. This means that we have a continuous floating upwards and down, a streaming upwards and down of spiritual beings of the higher hierarchies whose pupils, whose students, are the beings whose task it is to dispense the quick-ening forces for everything that sprouts and shoots in the course of the year. (GA 167, 11 April 1916)

With 'pupils of the higher hierarchies' we can surely understand 'Spirits of Cycles of Time', whose task it is to impart life-giving forces to the elemental beings.

As astral beings, the Spirits of Cycles of Time are closely connected to the astral bodies of animals and, above all, of human beings.

> Every time he sleeps, the human being dives with his astral body [into the world of these spirits], as though into a swelling sea. The nature of these beings is such that when someone becomes acquainted with them through occult vision, he experiences them as beings having something to do with his own soul, with his own astral body. They are beings whose influences on the human astral body—and also on the astral body of animals—are such that we can't speak only of a vitalizing effect, but of an effect like that of feelings, of thoughts, on our soul.... We can't say of these beings that they are in our environment, but when we perceive them {we see that} we are actually always united with them, as though poured into them. We merge into them and they speak to us in spirit. It is like perceiving thoughts and feelings from our surroundings; also will impulses, sympathies and antipathies come to expression in the thoughts, feelings and will impulses that flow from these beings towards us. So we can definitely see beings of this kind that are similar to the nature of the human soul. (GA 136, 4 April 1912)

In keeping with their high origin therefore, The Spirits of Cycles of Time have tasks of a far broader compass than those of the offspring of the second and third hierarchies, and employ the services of elemental beings to carry them out.

Apart from the Spirits of Cycles of Time there are still *other offspring of the first hierarchy* at work in earth existence. 'The higher spirits also have beings of this kind under them: the Spirits of Will have the undines; the Cherubim, sylphs; the Seraphim, salamanders.' (GA 121, 11 June 1910) With these beings that have 'detached' from the highest hierarchy we are presumably dealing with beings with stronger forces. Thus they could be the beings of energies which the first hierarchy radiate into the interior of the earth and cause to reflect or work back from there.

> Our planet is so constituted that the Spirits of Will or Thrones, the Cherubim, and Seraphim, all operate from its centre point.... We ascribe everything that we perceive when we gaze down into the depths of the earth to beings we have called the first hierarchy. (GA 121, 11 June 1910)

> What appears principally on our earth as the fluid element—although not indeed our present water but that ancient fluid element that has been brought to rest by the Spirits of Form—needs to be understood as the outer manifestation of the Spirits of Will or Thrones. But another element is always mixed in with this activity: assistance, so to speak, is given to the Spirits of Will or Thrones by the Cherubim and Seraphim. Help is given by the Cherubim in the element of air, in everything of an aeriform nature that permeates the apparent matter of the earth. Air is an illusion, so to speak, and behind it stand the mighty beings we call the Cherubim. The Seraphim are at work in what we know as warmth {or heat}, in everything that we find in the form of warmth. We see here what is caused in our planet by radiation outwards from its centre. (GA 121, 11 June 1910)

These first-hierarchy offspring, working from the interior of the earth, are of a different and more powerful nature than those of the second and third hierarchies that operate only at the etheric level. In Greek mythology, the beings active in the depths of the earth were called the 'lower gods'; they are the real creative divine beings who are connected with the dense physical elements which they constitute by means of their offspring. (GA 129, 25 August 1911, not quoted)

The beings of the first hierarchy are also evident, through yet another kind of offspring, in the periphery of the earth, in the atmospheric phenomena of cloud formation and lightning and thunder. The periphery is ruled by different laws than those on the surface and in the interior of the earth. What is evident here is that:

> in the amassing of clouds, in that unique process at the periphery of our earth whereby aeriform water vapour becomes water, the beings are at work that belong to the hierarchy of Cherubim. . . . We raise our gaze and see in the airy element—in which certainly the Spirits of Movement {also} hold sway—how the Cherubim are at work there so that the watery element, rising up out of the realm of the Spirits of Wisdom, condenses into clouds. The Cherubim govern the periphery of our earth just as much as Thrones, Spirits of Wisdom, and Spirits of Movement do within the earth's elemental existence. And when we now see the weaving and working of cloud formation itself, when we see what is hidden in its deeper nature as it were, and which announces its presence from time to time—that is the lightning and thunder that presses out from the cloud. For the seer, behind this activity lies the weaving and working of those spirits of the first hierarchy that we call the Seraphim. . . . Completely different forces are at work when the

element that rules in lightning, the electric element, emerges from matter; here the Seraphim hold sway. (GA 122, 22 August 1910)

However, not all the beings cited by Rudolf Steiner as the offspring of the first hierarchy are of a non-independent nature. He relates how originally there were only four Cherubic figures: the Lion, the Eagle, the Bull, and Man. But, 'fundamentally, each Cherubic figure had on its left and on its right a kind of progeny or companion. Think of each Cherubic figure with two companions, and then you have twelve forces and powers around the sun, whose presence was already hinted at in a certain way on Old Saturn. We have twelve powers of this kind belonging to the realm of Cherubim.' (GA 110, 13 April 1909) According to this, the progeny of the four chief figures also count as Cherubim. In passing, in reference to the group-ego of the minerals, we read: 'These spirits of Will, who belong to the first hierarchy (their offspring do not go so far as to be numbered among the first hierarchy), these Spirits of Will or their offspring give from themselves what becomes the group-ego of the minerals.' (GA 136, 14 April 1912)

This also seems to suggest that the offspring of the Spirits of Will are independent beings from which stem the lower group-souls of minerals. As a rule, however, beings referred to as offspring are of a non-independent nature.

8. The elementary kingdoms and the beings of the elemental world*

The similar names of the elementary kingdoms and the elemental beings of the elemental world already suggest the close connection between these two realms of being. The elemental world is essentially the same as the astral world. It encompasses the force-beings of the astral world that shape the physical world out of the astral level. These beings are etheric, so the elemental world therefore includes the realm of beings of the etheric world. The processes in human soul life are also connected with etheric energies, just as, on the other side, the etheric forces working at the physical level belong to the elemental world.

The elemental world is filled with thought-substance.

> What we have in our usual everyday consciousness is our thoughts. But this thought-world in itself is something quite different. And we do not understand the relation man has with his thoughts if we do not become aware of the nature of this thought-world itself. In reality, wherever we stand, walk or lie, we are not only in a world of air, light and so on, but we are always in a flowing world of thought. . . . Thought-substance fills the space around you. And this thought-substance is not a vague sea of thoughts, not something like a nebulous ether, but this thought-substance is actually what we call the elemental world. When we speak of beings of the elemental world, in the broadest sense of the word, then these beings consist of this thought-substance. (GA 177, 8 August 1917)

'In the broadest sense of the word' we are dealing here not only with elemental beings as such by themselves, but also with the thought-substance connected with them and of which they 'consist', as it were. This thought-substance can be none other than that of the elementary kingdoms which, as discussed, are the bearers of cosmic thought. And the connection of the elementary-kingdom beings with those of the elemental world is a particularly intimate one.

> Regarding these beings of the elemental world, the soul has the feeling that these beings have cosmic thoughts streaming into their individual

* Translator's note: Care is needed in this section to note when Kürten is referring to the elementary *kingdoms* or the elemental *world*—two distinct realms.

> existence, and that they *will* themselves in accordance with these in-streaming cosmic thoughts.... They experience their existence as something they give themselves through their will. In their thoughts on the other hand, they do not feel their thoughts to be something they produce themselves in the way man does; they feel their thoughts to be something that is given to them, as something that is not in themselves but in the world, and rays from the world into them. Thus these beings can never have any doubt that their thoughts are a reflection of the order poured out over the world as thought. They do not think *their* thoughts; they think *cosmic* thoughts. In their thinking, these beings live in cosmic thoughts; but they will themselves. Their feeling life is configured according to this willing and thinking. They feel themselves as a part of the cosmic whole; and they feel the necessity of willing themselves in a way that accords with this cosmic whole. (GA 17, 'Spiritual Beings')

The elemental beings absorb completely into their being the cosmic thoughts of the elementary kingdoms raying into them, will themselves through and in them, become one with them and are able to unfold their activity with them.

The beings of the elemental world are etheric beings. The ether too is described as being permeated with active thoughts. 'Ether is nothing other than a subtle substantiality that is permeated everywhere in such a way that flowing thought is active within it, that in reality thoughts outside fill the ether itself.... Then we reach a stage where we do not only perceive a surging life of thought in the ether, but in this surging thought-life we perceive real spirit beings.' (GA 66, 31 March 1917) These 'spirit beings' are evidently a reference again to the beings of the elementary kingdoms, whereas the elemental beings shape the 'subtle substantiality'. The spirit beings of the elementary kingdoms embody themselves as it were in the subtle substantiality of the ether—that is, in elemental beings. On one occasion Rudolf Steiner said that 'certain beings of the third elementary kingdom embody themselves on the astral plane in the warmth-beings that flow to and fro there as independent beings'. (GA 98, 4 December 1907)

Thus *the etheric beings of the elemental world are the bearers of the elementary kingdoms' formative forces of cosmic thought*. This also defines the nature of ether. *Ether is the elementary kingdoms' formative forces of thought borne by the beings of the elemental world*. Or more narrowly—if we consider the actual etheric world in the usual sense as distinct from the physical or astral worlds—ether is the second elementary kingdom's formative forces of thought, the thought forces of life, borne by the beings of the elemental world.

Elemental beings shape the phenomena of the physical world using elementary-kingdom forces of cosmic thought.

> The world of surging thoughts, which are not our thoughts but the thoughts in which we are immersed, this is the world from which our physical sense-perceptible world arises, rises up in condensed form so to speak.... Just as ice consists of the same substance as water but in a different state of aggregation, so our physical sense-perceptible world rises out of the surging, swelling sea of thought.... If we are to speak at all of what is 'behind physical reality', then we must speak of the objective weaving of thought, of the objective world of thoughts. (GA 181, 5 March 1918)

This 'objective world of thoughts' is the world of the elementary kingdoms.

The etheric body of the earth is composed of elemental beings. Cosmic ether streams into this etheric body from the widths of space, bearing to the earth the forces of cosmic thought. 'What is living in this raying-down to the earth are thoughts that everywhere create meaning (*sinnschöpferische Gedanken*). Cosmic ether is simultaneously a world of formative forces of thought.... When we experience how thoughts live in cosmic ether, they are not logical thoughts there, not thoughts such as have sharp contours: there they are picture-thoughts, images, imaginations.' (GA 84, 20 April 1923)

Connected with cosmic ether is the human etheric body which is the bearer of our thought-life. 'The activity of thinking, the connecting and separating of ideas, does not take place in the physical body but in the etheric or elemental body.' (GA 138, 31 August 1912) In usual human thinking, thoughts are passive, as it were; they can be joined together or separated quite arbitrarily. In the elemental world, thoughts are revealed as living beings with a life of their own. 'When with the clairvoyant soul we really live into the elemental world, then it is as though thoughts are not things that we manipulate, but become living beings.' (GA 147, 26 August 1913)

> The thoughts we get from the external sense-world and which we cart around with us through our waking consciousness are really thought-corpses, thoughts that have been paralysed and killed off. We are actually tied up in the thought-elemental world in such a way that in taking in our perceptions from the surrounding world and then pro-

> cessing these perceptions into thoughts, we kill the living thought. And we then think by virtue of having these thought-corpses in us. . . . We really walk around with our consciousness in such a way that we are carrying thought-corpses in ourselves, and call these thought-corpses our thoughts and mental images. (GA 177, 8 October 1917)

The thoughts we experience in our normal human consciousness are reflections in the physical body of the living thought-nature of the etheric body, and, as mere reflections, are without life or reality. In these reflected thought-images that can be manipulated at will, lies the surety of human freedom. For the human being can only become free in a thinking that has no reality and therefore cannot compel; only free thinking leads in time to free willing. (GA 4, not quoted)

The elemental beings' property of appearing as structures that are solid, fluid, and so on, evidently comes about by elemental beings absorbing into their own nature the thought-seed forces of the first elementary kingdom which shape the physical, by becoming one with them, by '*willing* themselves in accordance with these in-streaming cosmic thoughts'. By absorbing and uniting with the forces of shape and form with which cosmic thoughts are endowed, elemental beings become themselves the expression of these forces. So we can picture how certain elemental beings unite themselves with the specific forces of the first elementary kingdom that bring about the solid physical state, and thereby appear themselves at the elemental level as impenetrable beings. Other elemental beings absorb into their own nature those forces of the first elementary kingdom which at the physical level are the foundation of the watery, airy, and warmth conditions. Thus these elemental beings, connected as they are with first-elementary-kingdom forces of thought that shape the physical, become elemental formations without materiality, become the free-floating solid, fluid, aeriform, and warmth elements which, as supersensory entities, are not outwardly perceptible. These elemental conditions are 'the world from which our physical sense-perceptible world arises, rises up in condensed form, so to speak' through the elemental beings uniting themselves with the essential being of minerality. And the beings that live in these elemental forces and together with them manifest the physical sense-perceptible world, are the elemental beings: the fire beings (salamanders), air beings (sylphs), water beings (undines), and earth beings (gnomes)—the offspring of the beings of the third hierarchy and the Spirits of Form (section 7.2). It now becomes intelligible how, on the one hand, the living thought-beings of the elementary kingdoms acquire the ability to work formatively in the physical world, and, on the other hand, where the forces originate with which the elemental beings bring about formations at the physical level.

A more ancient humanity saw in the goddess Natura the creative power behind all phenomena of the sense-world which, in ancient times, was looked upon as a living world, and which still revealed itself to Greek initiates in their sleep. Such an initiate could speak of what had appeared to him in sleep: 'how forms are shaped, the forms of leaves, stems, the figuration of the world'. (GA 243, 14 August 1924) It was thus the configuration, the shaping of things, that was ascribed to the goddess Natura. So it was Natura who united the elementary kingdoms' shaping, formative forces of thought with the various elemental beings that served them.

Elemental beings belong to the lower sections of the physical plane.

In the physical world we distinguish:

solids,
liquids,
gases,
warmth-ether,
light-ether,
chemical-ether and
life-ether.

These are the seven levels of matter. (GA 93a, 4 October 1905)

Since warmth can express itself as both warmth-ether and physical heat, we get four lower and four higher sections of the physical plane. The active beings in these seven sections of the physical are referred to as 'etheric formative forces'.

Elemental beings comprise the lowest level of the elemental world. 'We know ... that the foundation of nature is the so-called elemental world for which we have names only if we go back to ancient mythology, in the various elemental beings which are behind the mineral realm as gnomes, behind the watery and plant world as undines, the enlivened aeriform realm as sylphs, and the whole earthly realm as salamanders.' (GA 167, 11 April 1916)

As a 'secretion' of the beings of the third hierarchy and of the Elohim (section 7.2) the elemental beings have no independence of their own. They consist, so to speak, only of body and soul; they have no essential spiritual core. Although they have a certain life and consciousness of their own, they are not responsible for what they do. They act instinctively, automatically, in accordance with the cosmic thought streaming into them from the elementary kingdoms and with the impulses from the higher beings who direct them. The consciousness of gnomes is wide-awake; they are entirely beings of intellect. By contrast, the consciousness of undines is dreamy, and that of sylphs more or less asleep. Salamanders live in a kind of deep-sleep consciousness.

The elemental beings are intended by higher powers for service in nature, and are connected for this purpose with the thought-seed forces of the first elementary kingdom. Thus they live in these cosmic thought-forces of the first elementary kingdom which stream into them, and which they take into their own natures as though in their life-element. By uniting themselves with the essential being of the mineral, and by impressing upon this their own attributes, making it an expression of their own nature, they bring about the things of the physical world. By letting go of the mineral level, they cause its phenomena to vanish again. Gnomes use life-ether to shape what is earthy-solid; undines use sound-ether to bring about the watery element; sylphs, the light-ether for the airy element; and salamanders, the warmth-ether for physical warmth.

Elementals are living beings. In the above discussion of the elemental world, warmth was described as being in the middle between an outwardly perceptible warmth and an inner soul warmth. When elemental beings connect with the mineral realm, their life is weakened, killed as it were, so that mineral structures appear without life.

Elemental beings are also active in the processes of nature as forces free of substance. Thus certain gnomes carry life-ether, 'in which they themselves live', to the roots of plants; undines bind and loose the substances of the air and bring them into the plant's leaves; sylphs permeate the plant with light; and salamanders preserve the seeds and germs of the kingdoms of nature. (GA 230, 2 November 1923, not quoted)

In the same way that elemental beings absorb into themselves the cosmic thoughts of the first elementary kingdom thus bringing about the phenomena of the physical world, so there are also other, higher elemental beings connected with the thought-seed forces of the *second elementary kingdom* which are the bearers of life. These are etheric beings in the strictest sense: the beings of warmth-, light-, sound-, and life-ether. In spiritual science, these beings are also ascribed to the physical plane. Thus, with reference to life-ether, we read that we are dealing here 'with the most rarefied physical state of all'. (GA 11, 'The Life of the Earth') After listing the seven levels of the physical plane, Rudolf Steiner added the following remark: 'Let's stay with the four lower levels of the physical plane, we'll keep the etheric world separate.' (GA 93a, 30 October 1905) Thus the actual etheric begins with the warmth-ether. The etheric beings of the higher sections of the physical plane are presumably the offspring of beings of the second hierarchy and of the Thrones.

The etheric bodies of plants, animals, and man are composed of warmth-, light-, chemical-, and life-ether. Thus the etheric body is also regarded as belonging to the physical even though it is supersensory. On one occasion Rudolf Steiner referred to it as the most rarefied matter—'what is beyond this [nerve substance] is the beginning of the supersensory levels where the human etheric body, which is supersensory, comes into consideration, which consists today of the finest material, {consists} of what manifests as the finest spray (*die feinsten Aussprühungen*) of the etheric, and is behind the material that is finer than nerve matter.' (GA 134, 30 December 1911)

Etheric beings are distinct from elemental beings primarily because, as the bearers of the life-forces of the second elementary level, they permeate plants, animals, and man with life—that is, with the capacity to keep their form internally mobile, and to change and reproduce out of themselves. Apart from this they do not connect directly with the mineral level but work on it by means of elemental beings for whom they are higher guides. Elemental beings operate according to physical laws; etheric beings, according to etheric laws.

> If we imagine the earth's forces spreading out from it on all sides, and the human being living in these forces that are those of the physical world, then we need to imagine the etheric world, proceeding from the great globe of the entire universe, the cosmos, approaching man from all sides, and meeting the physical forces. (GA 84, 22 April 1923)

All creatures on earth are placed within this polarity of the universal forces of ether working in levity from the cosmic periphery, and the forces of the physical working in gravity from the centre of the earth. Central forces have a pressing, compressing effect; universal forces a pulling, expanding one. The universal forces have more of an expansive effect in warmth- and light-ether, whereas the central forces working in chemical- and life-ether have more of a compressing effect*.

The etheric world is the world of unfolding life, of sprouting, budding and growth. Elemental warmth-ether is the living warmth which comes to expression for example in the warm blood of human beings, whereas mineral heat is a dead warmth. Light-ether is the element which, 'from

* This may not be quite correct. According to Ernst Marti, all four ethers work expansively as universal forces, whereas only central physical forces have a compacting effect. See *The Etheric—Volume I*, Dr Ernst Marti, Temple Lodge Publishing.

depths of spirit, weaving fruitfully in space, reveals the gods' creating'; at the same time it is the life element of all creatures on earth. Tone-ether is an echo of the harmony of the spheres; it causes the {chemical} binding and separating of substances and orders material existence according to number and measure. As sound-ether it facilitates the expression of thoughts in words. And what gives meaning to thoughts is carried by life-ether.

When we sleep, we dive into the elemental ether world with our physical and etheric bodies and draw enlivening forces from it. 'When we sleep, a relationship between the physical and etheric bodies is established with the whole cosmos, ...our physical and etheric bodies really live in what we call the elemental world, the world of pure forces.' (GA 159, 7 May 1915)

9. Influence of the elementary kingdoms on sleeping human beings

The formation of the subtle bodies in man by the elementary kingdoms is not a one-off event but a continuous process throughout human life because subtle bodies are constantly changing their form. Apart from this, the elementary kingdoms intervene significantly in human bodily nature during sleep.

When falling asleep, the human Ego and astral body separate in a certain sense from the physical and etheric bodies. The Ego and astral body are then in a supersensory world.

> This supersensory world is the three elementary kingdoms. . . . Just as the human being, when awake in the physical world, takes nourishment for his physical and etheric body from the kingdoms of nature, so the forces of the three elementary kingdoms flow into him between his falling asleep and waking up. This is now his arena. . . . Between falling asleep and waking up we are in the elemental world, . . . and we look out from this elemental world into the widths of the supersensory world and perceive angeloi, archangeloi and archai. ... However, the human being today, at the present stage of his development, does not directly have sufficient forces to integrate his Ego and astral body properly into the elemental world during sleep if he doesn't take spiritual knowledge into himself while awake. It is simply the case that what the human being received in a natural way in earlier times from the spiritual world, and what was helpful to him in the elemental world while asleep, is no longer received by him today from the elemental world. This is connected with the fact that he is to become a free being. . . .
>
> If you give [someone] some matter, a substance, let's say from the plant world, which is connected to a very specific elemental being, that person takes into his body something which gives his astral body a particular force as he enters the elemental world, so that he can find a connection to that particular elemental being, now as a soul-spiritual being. He brings this back with him when he awakens, and this has a health-giving effect. Actually, the health-giving effect does not come from the substance; what promotes health is the condition into which one puts the human being by means of the substance, by the substance

> having a relation to the elemental world, and transferring this relation with the elemental world onto the person. (GA 222, 12 March 1923)

It is the beings of the elementary kingdoms that build up and maintain the human members-of-being.

Something else also happens during sleep when the Ego and astral body are separated from the physical and etheric bodies and therefore cannot directly support them. The human being is dependent upon all his members-of-being working together; other forces, therefore, must take care of the physical and etheric bodies during sleep. This is also done by the elementary kingdoms.

The physical body, which first arose in germinal form on Saturn, was permeated and transformed in certain parts by each of the members-of-being that were subsequently added, so that this physical body today consists of four aspects which are each energized in a different way by the supersensory members, and given a particular characteristic by them. 'We know that the Ego finds its expression in the blood. In its motions, the blood is none other than the material manifestation of the I. Likewise, the nervous system is the material manifestation of the astral body, the glands are that of the etheric body, and the physical body has its own manifestation, so to speak.' (GA 98, 14 June 1908)

In its purely mineral parts the physical body works alone; in the blood, which is the particular expression of the Ego, all four subtle members are at work.

> The first bodily aspect into which all four members work is the red blood corpuscles. Wherever we have red blood, there we have all four members-of-being involved. The nerves are the second aspect. Wherever there are nerves, there the physical body, etheric body and astral body are involved. Wherever there are glands, there the physical and etheric bodies are involved. All the sense organs, all the physical apparatus in man, have only reached the stage of the mineral. They follow exactly the same laws as minerals. The eye and the ear belong to these mineral inclusions; there are also such components in the brain.... There are very specific parts of the fore-brain which are indeed pervaded by other radiations, but in which only mineral forces are at work. Things would get even more complicated if we were to look at the bones and muscles. When the Ego entered the human being, it began to develop the sentient-, intellectual-, and consciousness-soul, and it elaborated the bones and muscles. It takes years just to properly distinguish these things alone, if one wants to examine them carefully. One must investigate patiently, step by step. (GA 98, 4 December 1907)

What energizes, forms and shapes in this way the various parts of the physical body are the elementary kingdoms through which the subtle bodies operate.

While we are awake, the Ego and astral body operate in the blood, and the astral body in the nervous system. In order, therefore, to prevent the physical body from deteriorating during sleep, other forces must become active in place of Ego and astral body, and initially these are such forces as can take care of the blood in place of the Ego.

> You must ask yourself: what can we really know without clairvoyant perception? We can only know the mineral kingdom.... Initially the Ego can only manage to enliven the blood 'minerally', for it is unable to do more.... You look out with your senses, take in the laws of the mineral level, and impress these laws into the blood while you are awake. You push them into the blood in its totality. You enliven the blood in a mineral way. This is the real process that occurs in the act of knowing.... The laws of the mineral world ... do not stop in the sense organs but flow with the blood through the whole human body in the waking condition.
>
> ... The blood must be taken care of while we sleep. And because the blood is worked on at four levels, three other powers must intervene. First {there is} a power that is most closely related to the way in which our Ego works into the blood; this power is one that has not descended to the physical plane, ... {it is} an Ego that has remained above on the astral plane. This intervenes for the time being and takes over the work on the blood.... What [does it bring] into the blood? It brings what, since Saturn, has to be in the blood: fire, warmth. These are spirits ... who live on the astral plane and have a body of fire.... They move into the blood during the night and enliven it with their warmth.
>
> But since the blood is also deserted by the astral body, something else needs to happen. Beings must come also whose nature is such that they can work on the blood in the same way as the astral body does. These beings have their Ego in the spirit realm; this Ego has a much higher body that has not even condensed to the point of warmth.... It permeates the blood, doing in it the same as the astral body does during the day. The third Ego is in the [higher] spirit realm. (GA 98, 4 December 1907)

In this lecture Rudolf Steiner does not go into how the work of the astral body on the nervous system is substituted by other forces during sleep; these deputizing forces would likewise be from the elementary kingdoms. 'So you see how we are indeed sheltered and protected during the night by higher beings that do not live in the mineral realm, . . . they compose the hidden realms, the elemental realms that lie behind our physical world and work into it.' (GA 98, 4 December 1907)

In answer to a question at the end of the lecture, Rudolf Steiner then adds the following. 'The beings of the third elementary kingdom have similar needs to those of man. In the future they will also be on the physical plane. They are greedy to experience it, and are preparing to descend to the physical plane when human beings leave the physical plane at night as described earlier. They descend at night and acclimatize themselves so that soon they will be able to descend completely.' (GA 98, 4 December 1907) It is the life kernels of the animal kingdom which engage in formative activity at the present time as the third elementary kingdom.

In its present earthly existence, the human Ego can only grasp the mineral kingdom and impress its laws into the physical body. Man has to 'leave to the elementary kingdoms' the task of taking into his physical body the laws of the other kingdoms of nature. This means that, even while we are awake, the beings of the elementary kingdoms must take care of the laws of the other kingdoms of nature, apart from the mineral kingdom, in our physical body, as well as in the etheric and astral body. This was discussed in detail above in Chapter 3. Only during the further course of his development, or by developing higher vision, will man be able to take into himself additionally the laws of the other kingdoms of nature.

> You have often heard that the Ego works on the other bodies and transforms the astral body into spirit-self. To the degree that this occurs, the laws of the plant kingdom flow into the human nervous system. And when we attain the next level of clairvoyance, the laws of the animal kingdom flow into our glandular system. And when the human being works transformatively on the physical body, the laws of the human kingdom itself flow into the human body. (GA 98, 4 December 1907)

What we will be able to take into ourselves from the kingdoms of nature other than the mineral kingdom, and make use of only in the distant future—or even now through the {conscious} development of supersensory vision—must for the time being be taken care of even while we are awake by the elementary kingdoms working together with the group-egos of the natural kingdoms. There is an enormous amount going on in the human being of which he is normally quite unaware. But a knowledge of it will become increasingly necessary for him in the future if he wishes to establish himself properly in his earthly life and his destiny, as the following will show.

The elemental beings that exert an influence on the human members-of-being are of course directed, however, by beings of the higher hierarchies who operate in man in the greatest variety of ways. As a consequence, the relationships show themselves to the seer very differently depending on the point of view from which he perceives and describes them. We discussed in Chapter 4 the close connection of the beings of the third hierarchy to the human members-of-being which are extensions as it were of the realms of these higher beings. In a different context Rudolf Steiner said that every time we sleep our human blood and nervous system are taken care of by 'the same beings who on Old Saturn caused the first germinal condition of the physical body to arise, and who formed the etheric body on Old Sun'—in other words, by the Thrones and the Spirits of Wisdom. (GA 104, 19 June 1908) Elsewhere we read that when we sleep the organs that have been deserted by the Ego are supported by beings of the third hierarchy, and organs deserted by the astral body are supported by beings of the second hierarchy. And not only when we sleep, but also while we are awake, the beings of the first, the highest hierarchy, live in our etheric body. And likewise the powers of the Trinity, the powers of the Father, the Son, and the Spirit, live in the physical body. (GA 228, 2 September 1923, not quoted)

This gives us a picture of the influences of higher beings in man that is difficult to encompass in its details, but which, in so far it is dealing with the influences of formative forces, is mediated by the beings of the elementary kingdoms.

The intervention of forces from extra-human beings in the bodily members of the sleeping human being has further significant consequences. Rudolf Steiner speaks of this in lectures in which he is not explicitly talking about beings of the elementary kingdoms, but of elemental beings. Yet here too we are evidently dealing with beings of the elementary kingdoms, who are connected with elemental beings. We saw above that it is clearly the beings of the elementary kingdoms that inhabit the subtle bodies of the sleeping human being. Thus Steiner refers to the beings that move in to our members-of-being at night when we sleep as beings 'that find themselves in the higher worlds', as 'beings from higher realms', as 'higher, protective spirits', through whom man is 'taken care of by higher worlds'. 'Astral entities, which create the physical and etheric bodies, which took part in their creation, take them on again when the human being leaves them.' (GA 98, 14 June 1908) This all suggests that both here and on occasions elsewhere (see Chapter 8) 'elemental beings' means the beings of the elementary kingdoms that are connected with them.

Another consideration follows from this. After he had described in the first part of the lecture the working of 'elemental beings' on the sleeping human being, Rudolf Steiner turns briefly towards the end of the lecture to the actual elemental beings, the gnomes and so on, which work as forces of nature. He says, 'The spiritual worlds express themselves in many other kinds of beings as well.... We can mention the elemental beings.' (GA 98, 14 June 1908) We can also conclude from this that the elemental beings spoken about in the first part of the lecture are not the same as these 'other kinds', but the beings of the elementary kingdoms. These elementary kingdoms—behind which naturally stand the higher, divine-spiritual beings—have shaped the physical and etheric body, and they are the ones who also take care of these members-of-being while we sleep.

> When these beings enter the members of the sleeping human being, they find {the bodies} to be different from how they were when they were first bestowed on man by these beings. While awake, people have been in the physical and etheric body with their astral body and Ego, and have been busy there. And the spiritual beings from higher cosmic realms find effects there that in no way correspond with their own high spirituality, that are the after-effects of what people's astrality and Ego have inflicted on the physical body during the day.... We cannot have any thought, any sensation or feeling, without this having an effect right into the physical body and causing a certain change in its structure.
>
> Of particular significance are the effects left in the *physical body* by everything that people have in their souls by way of lies, calumnies, hypocrisy.... And we are not talking here only of the soul experiences which we call lies in a blatant sense, but also the refined, conventional lies like those, for example, that become necessary just by the way society is today. Lying to be polite or from good behaviour and the whole gamut that could be cited of dishonesty and hypocrisy and little calumnies, even just in thought—all this is expressed as effects on the physical body, and this is what these descending beings find there. And this causes ... something very particular to happen. This causes pieces to be constantly torn away from the substance of these beings who descend into the body. Certain parts of the higher beings have to become detached because of this, ... which thereby have a certain relationship to the human physical body. These {now-detached} entities consequently attain an independent existence in the spiritual

> world around us; they are entities that we class as *phantoms*. Phantoms are spiritual entities which in their appearance are physiognomic expressions, copies in a certain sense, of the human body and form. They consist of such a fine materiality that the physical eye cannot see them, but they nevertheless have a physical form, so to speak. The clairvoyant sees pieces of human heads, human hands, whole shapes, swarming through the air, he even sees internal parts of human bodies, the stomach, the heart—he sees all the phantoms which have become detached due to the human being passing on to his physical body the results of lies, hypocrisy, and calumny. (GA 98, 14 June 1908)

In another lecture we find additionally:

> Because of this something new happens, something completely new is created. Entities are detached from the higher beings by the physical body, which then lead an independent existence between our worlds.... They are called phantoms because they are the closest to physical perception. They are beings that are also subject to physical laws. They whirr through our space. They hold up human development. They make things in the world worse than they would be without them.... Phantoms are a kind of nature being that exists due to having been created by man. The human being leaves his physical body at night, leaving behind in it the imprint of lies, hypocrisy, and so on. When he enters it again in the morning, these phantoms first stream out of the physical body. (GA 98, 9 June 1908)

As we see, these 'detachments' are made from the 'substances' of the beings that enter the physical body. Among those beings that form the physical body and take care of it during the night, there are also beings belonging to the first elementary kingdom. They are the life kernels of the minerals connected to the living thought-beings of the lowest region of spirit land. These living thought-beings are the substance in which the life kernels clothe themselves. It would therefore seem to be living thought-beings of the physical level that detach themselves from the beings of the first elementary kingdom and attain an independent existence as copies of human bodily limbs and organs, under physical laws. It surely cannot be assumed that parts are detached from the high and highest divine-spiritual beings themselves, who work down into the human being through lower beings that serve them. These detached parts from the beings of the elementary kingdoms are presumably also carried by actual elemental beings, which is why Rudolf Steiner refers to them as elemental beings. Thus in a later lecture, speaking about these detachments, he says that these entities are detached 'from the spiritual world' and that we have in them 'a certain group of elemental beings that are related to our physical body'. (GA 120, 4 June 1908)

These phantoms work in a highly unfavourable way into human life.

> In a certain sense they have intelligent attributes but no moral responsibility. They spend their existence putting obstacles in the way of peoples' lives.... Important sources of sickness are to be found in entities of this kind, since if these phantoms are created by people, they find a very good opportunity for their existence in bacilli and bacteria, they find nourishment in them, as it were.... But these bacteria are also created by them in a certain way. (GA 98, 14 June 1908)

Also in the human *etheric body* there are,

> effects that are made by certain processes of our soul life which are still there during the night and then cause entities along the lines of the etheric body to detach from what has descended and entered {the body}. The soul processes that lead to entities of this kind are those that arise in human community through what we can call bad laws, wrong measures. Everything wrong that the soul experiences with regard to the effects of laws between one human being and another, exerts an effect on the soul such that in the night an after-effect of it remains bringing about a detaching of the entities we call *spectres*. This is a second species of entity belonging to those created by man. (GA 98, 14 June 1908)

> Factors that have a bad effect on the etheric body are things, for example, like bad laws or bad social institutions in a community. Everything that leads, for example, to discontent, that acts as a bad social condition between one person and another, has an effect that extends into the etheric body by the mood it creates in the individuals of a community.... So, for someone who is able discern these things spiritually, there can be many people going about amongst us whose physical body is 'larded', we could say, with phantoms, and whose etheric body is 'larded' with spectres or ghosts. And all this scatters as a rule after death, or shortly thereafter, and populates the world. (GA 102, 4 June 1908)

> Entities that arise due to bad laws lead people into making more bad laws. (GA 98, 9 June 1908)

These ghosts or spectres that are formed 'along the lines of the etheric body', receive their form from the second elementary kingdom which is the architect of the etheric body. These entities are presumably also living thought-beings which become detached from the beings of the second elementary kingdom and are carried by elemental beings.

In the same way, imprints in the human *astral body* can become the cause of parts detaching from the higher beings that enter the astral body, and which then wreak harm in the world as *demons*.

> The way the astral body is organized means that it needs to be integrated in the nervous system. When it is outside, it is not in its rightful place and it too must be taken care of by higher worlds; higher, protective spirits must connect with it. And detachments can also arise from these beings due to human soul activity. (GA 98, 14 June 1908)

These detachments from beings who take care of the human astral body during sleep are caused by everything that disregards the dignity and freedom of the human soul.

> Just think how for the most part the soul today wants to overpower its fellow souls, how it can't bear it when another soul thinks or loves something else, how one soul wants to dominate and influence the other. In everything that works in our world from one soul to another, from the unjustified piece of advice that one gives, to all the techniques people use to dominate others; in everything that doesn't act so that one free soul stands before another free soul, but, and even in the smallest way, uses coercive means to convince, coercive means to persuade; where one doesn't just try to awaken what is slumbering in the other soul—in all this forces work from soul to soul in such a way that their influence in these souls is expressed in the astral body during the night. The astral body is influenced, and because of this entities are detached from other worlds that now whirr through our world as elemental beings. These entities can be classified as demons. They only exist because intolerance of thought is exercised in our world in the most varied forms. (GA 102, 4 June 1908)

> When something like this happens, it harms the astral body of both individuals.... These demonic entities have a particularly adverse influence on our human development. They whirr through spiritual space and prevent people from developing their personal view.... There is no other means for the human being to free himself from the influence of these harmful spiritual entities than by a knowledge of these facts, and by being aware of what he is doing. (GA 98, 9 June 1908)

These demons, it would seem, are living thought-beings detached from beings of the third elementary kingdom and connected with elemental beings.

Rudolf Steiner also classifies spirits of the lie as demons.

> Since lie-demons of this kind are always created by the great personalities of world history, and grow into very powerful entities, we refer to them as 'spirits of hindrance {or obstruction}', or as 'hindrances'.... Thus there is a form of bacillus which is the carrier of infectious diseases, that originates from the lies of human beings. It is nothing other than embodied lie-demons. We see here how the lies of ancient times arise in world karma as armies of entities. Just how much truth there is in myths and sagas can be seen in a particular place in *Faust.* A connection is made there between vermin and lies, and also in the role played by rats and mice in connection with the spirit of lies, Mephistopheles. There are often wonderful connections in sagas between the spiritual and physical world. (GA 99, 30 May 1907)

> All these entities—phantoms, spectres, and demons—work back again on the human being. When a prejudice arises like an epidemic around us, or an absurd fashion of some kind, this is the work of demons, created by people, who are holding up all the straight lines of progress. The entities people create always whirr and spin around them. People are always surrounded by the web of beings they have created, and which whirr around them. (GA 98, 14 June 1908).

Our task in the future will be to transform these demons, spectres, and phantoms 'into servants of a progressive evolution'. (GA 98, 9 June 1908). From all this it is evident that, also in this respect, the human being is closely bound up with the elementary kingdoms.

Elemental beings of various kinds also work from the planets into the earth and man. They are both good and bad beings, belonging to the astral and devachanic planes, that have their home on one of the planets; their influence, however, extends to the earth. Thus people who suffer from delusions, also mediums and sleepwalkers, are under the influence of astral moon beings of this nature. Where love and goodwill unfold in human life, benevolent Mars beings are also involved. Certain inventive Saturn beings are also involved in human inventions, in technology for example. In actions that require presence of mind, Venus beings are involved. Other Saturn beings that slide into the human being through sense impressions—through seeing, hearing, smell and so on—unleash passions in him of a sensual nature.

Astral-elemental beings of the planets are also active in human organs. Crowds of the moon and Mars beings mentioned above live in the lymph, and influence people's character. Both benevolent and malevolent devachanic Venus beings live in digestive chyle, and work additionally in the earth's plant life, thus also exposing people to the influence of these beings in their food. Saturn beings have a strong influence on the liver. We would have to regard all these elemental beings of the planets as being of a non-independent nature, as separated off from higher beings. To what extent there is a distinction in these beings, according to their type and origin, between the active cosmic thoughts in them and the elemental beings of the earth plane, must remain an open question. Thus:

> in the most varied situations of life the human being is constantly surrounded and whirred-about by elemental beings of this kind, as they are also called. He is truly never alone. Whatever he does or undertakes is at the same time the opportunity and cause for the development of a number of entities. People's refined and coarse acts, the most ideal and idealistic and the most terrible actions, are all the causal occasion for the presence of creatures of this kind that intervene in human forces and operate there. And we must know them if we really want to understand life. (GA 102, 6 January 1908)

10. The elementary kingdoms as hidden predisposition in the human members-of-being

We see a direct relationship between the human members-of-being and those of the mineral, plant, and animal, in the fact that the bodies relating to one another here are shaped by the same elementary kingdoms: the physical body by the first kingdom, the etheric body by the second, and the astral body by the third. However, there is another hidden relationship of a different kind between human subtle bodies and those of the kingdoms of nature, which is different from the relationship just mentioned. With the exception of the physical body, the human members have, *as a predisposition*, the forms of the kingdoms of nature, and the inclination to copy these forms in themselves; they are prevented from doing so, however, by the human constitution as a whole. Thus the human etheric body bears within itself all the forms of the animal kingdom, the astral body bears those of the plant kingdom, and the Ego-structure those of the mineral kingdom. For example, when someone has an animal before him, his etheric body is inclined to take on the form of that animal.

> Just as we have air around us, we also have in our surroundings the forces that give the creatures of the animal kingdom their forms. And these forces also work on people. . . . All the forms [of the animal kingdom] are in our etheric bodies as a predisposition, and we can only understand these forms by inwardly imitating them as it were. It is only our physical body that prevents us from taking on these forms. So we can say that we actually carry the whole animal kingdom in ourselves, in our etheric body. . . .
>
> Likewise we are surrounded by the same realm of forces that give forms to plants. Just as our etheric body is predisposed to take on all animal forms, so is our astral body predisposed to imitate all plant forms. . . . Our astral body is thoroughly ensouled with the tendency to fall in line with the forces that come to expression in plant form. Thus we can say: the astral body reacts to the complex of forces that give plants their form. . . . The mineral kingdom: this in turn is a complex of forces that gives the various minerals their forms. This works in our Ego. We see this very clearly in the Ego, since everything you think is mineral kingdom. . . . So our Ego is living in this complex of forces that

> shapes the mineral kingdom.... The physical body as such doesn't live in any kingdom, it is a kingdom in itself.... We are only human in our physical body.... From this perspective, the animal kingdom is connected to the etheric body, the plant kingdom to the astral body, and the mineral kingdom to the Ego. (GA 199, 3 September 1920)

Elsewhere we find that if the human etheric body were not held together by the physical, it would disintegrate into separate pieces, all of which would represent together the entire animal kingdom.

> In earlier, prehistoric times, when evolution was at a different stage, the human form as a whole was dispersed over the many animals.... The forces that are spread over this animal kingdom were extracted, as it were, and are still present in our etheric body. [And in our astral body there is everything] that is spread over the world as the manifold forms of the plant kingdom. [It is] held together only by the elasticity of the physical and etheric bodies. [And from our Ego] we would get the whole picture of the mineral world with all its many secrets of the cosmos. We have, contracted in this Ego, what is otherwise spread out over the whole cosmos. We bear the mineral cosmos within us. (GA 167, 25 April 1916)

Rudolf Steiner states the same thing in a different way when he connects with the head system the tendency to imitate animal forms; the tendency to imitate the plant kingdom he connects with the torso system; and the tendency to imitate mineral crystal forms, with the limb system. (GA 293, 3 September 1919, not quoted) This is connected with the fact that, bodily, the Ego is bound up with the limb system; the astral body, with respect to the organs through which it works, is connected to the torso system; and the etheric body, with respect to its bodily aspect, to the head system. (GA 175, 6 March 1917, not quoted)

A consequence of these forces seated as disposition in the human subtle bodies, would be that, after death, an entire etheric animal kingdom would have to arise from the etheric body, and a supersensory plant kingdom from the astral body, if this were not prevented by the intervention of higher divine-spiritual beings. (GA 174a, 20 March 1916, not quoted)

In his evolution, man has passed through the mineral, plant, and animal kingdoms, and is now at the human stage. From this passage through the kingdoms of nature man retained certain forces that are now active in these kingdoms. Behind the physical forms of minerals, plants, and animals are the formative forces of the cosmic thought of the first elementary kingdom with which, during successive embodiments of the earth, man too has shaped his physical body. It is supposedly these formative forces of the first elementary kingdom in the individual planetary conditions that have remained from earlier stages as predisposition in the human members-of-being. The first elementary kingdom was formed during the Saturn period by primordial human beings in connection with the thought-seed entities of the upper region of spirit land; in the Sun period, by primordial animal being; in the Moon period, by primordial beings of 'plant-ness'; and in the Earth period, by the primordial beings of the mineral kingdom. With these formative forces of primordial beings constituting the first elementary kingdom, and during the evolution of earth's embodiments prior to the present one—which were briefly repeated at a higher level at the beginning of earth evolution,—the human physical body was formed in such a way that the highest subtle member at each stage determined the form of the physical level. In other words, the physical body was always the expression of this highest member. (See Chapter 4)

In present Earth existence, the Ego as the highest member of man's being fashions the physical body using the formative forces of the mineral kingdom which is now the first elementary kingdom. The Ego had to assimilate these formative forces, make them its own, in order to be able to shape its physical and mineral form by means of them. The mineral kingdom expresses itself at the physical level in the formation of crystal forms. So the Ego bears within itself this ability of shaping crystalline forms. It would also fashion the physical body in these crystal forms if the physical body did not have to arise in human form as the expression of the Ego. Because the Ego bears within itself the formative forces of the mineral kingdom, however, it is able to reproduce inwardly the mineral forms it perceives in the external world.

During the ancient Moon period it was the astral body, as the highest human member-of-being, that shaped the physical body by means of the formative forces of the first elementary kingdom. During this moon period, the first elementary kingdom was the plant realm. The astral body fashioned the physical body using these plant-kingdom formative forces, not, however, in plant form but, as the expression of the astral body, in man-animal form, since human beings were then at the animal stage. The astral body has preserved the ability and inclination, brought over from the Moon period, to shape plant forms.

During the ancient Sun period the human organism consisted of physical and etheric body. Being the higher member, the etheric body shaped the physical body using the formative forces of the animal kingdom which, during Old Sun, were the first elementary kingdom. The physical body of humanity on Old Sun, however, did not have animal form, but, being the expression of the etheric body, had plant form. Humanity was at that time at the plant stage. The ability and inclination to create animal forms, however, has been brought over from the Old Sun period and preserved in the etheric body.

During the Old Saturn period man himself lived in the first elementary kingdom and thus formed his physical body with his own formative forces. For this reason the physical body of humanity on Old Saturn received no formative forces other than human ones, and these human form tendencies have remained in the physical body in subsequent times.

To summarize we can say: on Old Saturn man shaped his physical body as a physical (mineral) being using the formative forces of his own human kingdom in mineral form; on Old Sun, as an etheric (plant-like) being using the formative forces of the animal kingdom in plant form; on Old Moon, as astral (animal-like) being using the formative forces of the plant kingdom in animal form; and during the earth period, as spiritual being (Ego-being) using the formative forces of the mineral kingdom in human form.

The form tendencies of the first elementary kingdom that each time shaped the physical body, continue even now as hidden predisposition in the human members-of-being. This helps us understand the origin of these predispositions which, though unable to unfold, enable the human being inwardly to copy or imitate the forms of minerals, plants, and animals, and thus understand them.

10.1 *The relation of the elementary kingdoms to the lower human members-of-being and to the third hierarchy*

Just as man forms the lower and higher members of his being using the formative forces of the elementary kingdoms, so the beings of the third hierarchy also work with these forces in the process of spiritualizing their own lower members. This results in many different relationships between the subtle anatomy of archai, archangels, and angels, and the corresponding human members. The human physical body is fashioned and maintained by the first elementary kingdom, the etheric body by the second, and the astral body by the third. These elementary kingdoms stand under the directorship of the beings of the third hierarchy in whose consciousness they rested in the beginning of the physical Stage of Form in the earth's evolution, and from whose consciousness they were released during the course of it. During the Earth period, the elementary kingdoms work through the elemental beings of the solid, liquid, and gaseous levels. Elemental beings are the 'offspring' of the beings of the third hierarchy. This clarifies why the human physical body is governed by the archai, the etheric body by the archangels, and the astral body by the angels. These human members-of-being are components, extensions in a certain sense, of the subtle members of the higher beings in question.

> It is truly the case that the physical form we receive at birth and lay aside at death comes from the realm of the archai, the Primal Beginnings, the Primal Forces. In other words, we actually have our physical form because we are encompassed by a spirit of the realm of archai. We are inside a spirit that was in the realm of the archai and which now {at our death} draws back again what it had lent us during our lifetime. . . . This form provides further nourishment . . . for a spirit from the hierarchy we call the archai. . . .
>
> If we look now at the second member of the human being, the human etheric body, it is also the case here that we certainly cannot talk of this as of something belonging completely to ourselves, but rather, in the same way as the physical form actually belongs to the realm of archai and we are clothed in an extension of the realm of archai, so with regards to our etheric body we are clothed in an extension of the realm of archangels, of archangeloi. Thus we can say: when we pass through the portal of death, we keep this etheric body for a short while. We know that it then dissolves. But this dissolution doesn't mean that is disappears into nothingness, but rather it returns to the realm of archangeloi. They in turn have certain requirements regarding it. They lower, as it were, a part of their being into the earthly realm of human beings, and constitute thereby the human etheric body during its lifetime. . . .
>
> And with regards to our astral body, a similar relationship exists between it and the realm of angeloi, of angels. . . . Our astral body is also not entirely our own; it is an extension of the angel beings. So we can say: at death, something goes over from the human astral body into the realm of angeloi. We also have our astral body as a clothing of our being from the realm of the angeloi. (GA 205, 17 July 1921)

Steiner is speaking here expressly about the physical *form*, and also the form of the etheric and astral body, which are activated by the elementary kingdoms. The archai work with the formative forces of the first elementary kingdom on the spiritualization of their own physical body into spirit-man, and at the same time on the human physical body. The arising of the human etheric and astral body from the realm of archangels and angels is explained in the same way. This applies however only to the overall shaping of the subtle bodies, since these consist of many different aspects, and different hierarchies operate in these aspects through their offspring. Thus for example, the human physical body is composed of a solid, a watery, a gaseous, and a warmth aspect.

> The physical organism is initially just itself, it is the physical body.... We cannot look at [the fluid organism] without thinking of it being permeated by the etheric body. Thirdly, we have the airy organism. We cannot consider this without thinking of it being energized through and through by the astral body. Fourthly and finally we have the highly differentiated warmth organism. We cannot consider this without finding it energized throughout by the I.... And when we consider our organism, we find a complete etheric organism consisting of chemical-ether, warmth-ether, light-ether, and life-ether. (GA 202, 17 December 1920)

It follows from this that only the solid part of the physical body is governed by the archai alone; in other parts other beings collaborate with them through their offspring. So we can say: in the solid components of the physical body—those permeated by physical forces alone—the archai are working through their offspring, the gnomes, with the formative thought-seed forces of the first elementary kingdom. In the fluid organism of the physical body, which is energized by the etheric, the archai collaborate with the archangels who, through their offspring, the undines, work with the formative thought-seed forces of the second elementary kingdom. In the airy organism of the physical body, which is energized by the astral level, the angels, through their offspring, the sylphs, collaborate with the archai using the formative thought-seed forces of the third elementary kingdom. In the warmth organism of the physical body, which is energized by the Ego-related and spiritual level, the human being himself works with the thought forces of the fourth elementary kingdom through the salamanders, the offspring of the Spirits of Form.

The mineral aspect of the human physical body is shaped by the archai; the plant aspect in the physical body, by the archangels; the animal aspect, by the angels; and the actual human aspect, the Ego-related spiritual level, by man himself.

Rudolf Steiner refers in another connection to this formation of the human physical body by the archai, and his etheric body by the archangels. Our human predecessors, in the way they arose on Saturn, Sun, and Moon, did not yet have a uniform shape. Only during the earth period were the various human forms united into the present common form.

> The hierarchy of Primal Forces {archai} saw it as their task to bring pre-human human beings—whose soul life likewise corresponded to their one-sided formations—to a single, common human form. Humanity was passed to them by the exusiai. In thought, the exusiai had already created a human unity out of plurality. But with the exusiai this unity was still an ideal form, a form in cosmic thought. The archai shaped the etheric form from it, but in such a way that this etheric form already contained the forces needed to bring about the physical form. Something tremendous is revealed when we look at this situation: the human being is an ideal of the gods and an aim of the gods.... The fact that man can integrate himself in an upright position into the gravitational conditions of the earth; that within these gravitational conditions he can maintain his balance in free movement; that he can tear his arms and hands free from gravity and use them in freedom—all this we have, and much more besides that lies within us but is structure nevertheless, thanks to this creation by the hierarchy of archai. (GA 26, during New Year 1925, Part 1)

> [Then with regard to the etheric body he says:] The hierarchy of archangels gives to man's etheric body that which corresponds in it to the form of the physical body, which man has thanks to the archai.... The earth lives in the physical body, and the starry world in the etheric body. The inner forces that man bears within himself in order to exist on the earth, with which at the same time he frees himself from the earth through his {upright} posture, movement, gesture—these he has thanks to the creative work of the archangels in his etheric body. Just as earthly forces live in the physical body through formation, so forces streaming in from all sides of the surrounding cosmos live in the etheric body. (GA 26, during New Year 1925, Part 1)

When, from another angle, Rudolf Steiner speaks of the archai as being active in the present human Ego, the archangels in the astral body, and the angels in the etheric body, there is no contradiction to what has been said above concerning the relation of the archai to the human physical form, of the archangels to the form of the etheric body, and of the angels to the form of the astral body. The forces of the elementary kingdoms, with which the beings of the third hierarchy shape human subtle bodies, are formative in nature. What happens in these subtle bodies as inner experience, and in which the beings of the third hierarchy also participate, is something different. The inner connection between the human form and the Ego is already given by the form being a complete expression of the Ego. (GA 161, 9 January

1915, not quoted) Concerning the connection of the archai with the human I, Rudolf Steiner says:

> On Saturn, in order to live at all, they [the archai] needed the physical substance which was at the same time the rudiment of human substance; on Sun they needed the etheric substance which was poured out to become man's etheric body; on Moon, the astral substance. Here on the earth, they need our I. (GA 107, 19 June 1909)

'I' is referring here to the fourth component of our being, the Ego-structure of man. It is not the formative aspect that is being spoken about here, but of what these beings of the third hierarchy experience for themselves through the human members-of-being. On Saturn, through the rudiment of the human physical form, the archai develop their Ego-consciousness; on Sun, through the human etheric body, they develop their Imaginative consciousness; on Moon, through the human astral body, they develop their Inspirative consciousness; and during the present Earth evolution, through the Ego-structure of human beings, they develop their Intuitive consciousness.

A similar process applies to the relation of the archangels and angels to the members of our being. The archangels attained their Ego-consciousness through the human physical body on Old Sun; their Imaginative consciousness through the human etheric body on Old Moon; and in the present Earth evolution, the human astral body serves them in their attainment to Inspirative consciousness.

The angels too, who attained their Ego-consciousness on Moon, needed the human physical body for that process, just as, at present, they need the human etheric body to develop their Imaginative consciousness.

While using human members-of-being for their own development, these beings at the same time activate processes in these members over which man as yet has no power. The being of humanity thus reveals itself as a shared organ of the gods, as the temple of the gods.

Regarding the attainment, through the members of man's being, of the various levels of consciousness in the beings of the third hierarchy and in man, we need to keep in mind that these members-of-being are in turn composed of different parts, and only certain of these parts serve the development of the various kinds of consciousness. They are those parts of our being which arise during each embodiment of the earth and are not transformed later by the addition of other members-of-being. For, as discussed earlier, the higher members create their own expression in the lower members by partially transforming them.

The human physical body received its first rudiments on Saturn.

During the Sun period the etheric body was integrated into this, which permeated a part of the physical body with life forces. In this part, etheric forces worked together with physical ones, while in the remaining part only physical forces were at work. During the Moon period, the astral body was added, which likewise permeated a part of the physical body which now consisted of three parts. In the same way, during the Earth period, the Ego has created its expression in a part of the physical body. This is therefore composed at present of four different parts. (GA 98, 4 December 1907, not quoted) In the part that has remained purely physical, the forces of the first elementary kingdom work alone; in the Sun-part the forces of the first and second kingdom; and in the Moon-part, all three elementary kingdoms together. In the part of the physical body permeated by the Ego, man's own elementary kingdom works together with the other three.

In the same way, the etheric and astral body have also become differentiated during the course of evolution. In the Sun-part of the etheric body, its own etheric forces work alone; in the Moon-part of the etheric body the astral body is also at work; and in the Earth-part there is additionally the Ego. In the Moon-part of the astral body, the astral works alone, whereas in the Earth-part it works together with the Ego.

From this perspective, and looked at more precisely, the being of man thus consists of ten parts: four parts of the physical body, three parts of the etheric body, two parts of the astral body, and the Ego. These various parts of the human organism should naturally not be thought of as separate but as fully interpenetrating one another. Such is the complexity of the earthly body of man!

Only the Saturn-part of the physical body served the beings of the third hierarchy—and present-day man—to attain Ego-consciousness. The Sun-part of the etheric body successively enabled archai, archangels, and angels to attain their Imaginative consciousness; the Moon-part of the astral body enabled the archai and archangels to attain Inspirative consciousness; and by means of the Ego-structure, the earth-part of humanity, the archai develop their Intuitive consciousness.

Man in present earth development thus consists of a Saturn-man, a Sun-man, a Moon-man, and an Earth-man. While awake, the human being experiences himself as an Ego-being *by means of* the Saturn-part of his physical body; this Saturn-part reflects back, as it were, his inner experiences, just as on Old Saturn the archai attained their Ego-consciousness by 'the warmth of Saturn reflecting back this "I" and bringing it to consciousness'. However, what is experienced *in* this Saturn-man when we form our conscious mental pictures, is still veiled for us in a dull, deep-sleep consciousness. We sleep through what we experience in our Sun-man, and dream through what we experience in our Moon-man. These processes, which for us remain in the unconscious parts of our being, are experienced consciously by the beings of the third hierarchy. 'What the Moon-man dreams, the angelos Imagines. . . . What the Sun-man experiences in a sleeping state, the archangelos Inspires. . . . What the Saturn-man is in deep sleep, the Spirit of Personality Intuits.' (GA 162, 3 June 1915)

What human beings experience only subconsciously in these parts of their nature, forms, through the fact that the beings of the third hierarchy experience it consciously, the seeds for future Jupiter.

> We bear a Saturn-man in ourselves. But because this Saturn-man is integrated into the activity of the Spirits of Personality, he is the seed for Jupiter. Jupiter will have to attain what will be its mineral foundation from what we bear within ourselves as Saturn-man. . . . What our Sun-man experiences with a sleeping consciousness will have matured at the end of the earth period to the point of being able to render up cosmic impulses for the plant world on Jupiter, through the archangeloi. . . . The dream images of our Moon-man (or of the dreamer in man), will on Jupiter become condensed Imaginations comprising the basis of an animal kingdom, through the angeloi. . . . The mental pictures of our Earth-man will become impulses for humanity's evolution on Jupiter, through the soul content of the most highly developed human beings. (GA 162, 3 June 1915)

Thus humanity unconsciously bears the seeds, nurtured by the beings of the third hierarchy, of future evolution, and will itself develop such seeds during the further course of earth's development, in full consciousness. And all these seeds are those of the elementary kingdoms from which the realms of being on the Jupiter embodiment of the earth will also be shaped.

What has been said above regarding the various connections of the beings of the third hierarchy with the human members-of-being also applies to their connections to the members-of-being of the kingdoms of nature. Here too we must make a distinction between the formative shaping of the members and the essential being of the mineral, plant, and animal that lives in these forms. The shaping of their members occurs through the beings of the third hierarchy using the forces of the elementary kingdoms, in the same way as with man. The physical body is formed by the archai using the forces of the first elementary kingdom; the etheric body of plants and animals, by the archangels using the forces of the second elementary kingdom; and the astral body of animals, by the angels using the forces of the third elementary kingdom.

The relationship of the third hierarchy to the essential being of the kingdoms of nature is different from their relationship to the formative processes in these kingdoms. This is connected to the fact that the essential being of the natural kingdoms was originally also carried in the consciousness of these higher beings, and then released by them, but in a different way from how this took place with regard to the forms of the members-of-being. When earth development entered its present, fourth Stage of Life, to begin with only humanity appeared as independent life-seeds on the arupa plane. These had previously rested in the consciousness of the archai. There was an early period in the evolution of the earth 'during which, when one looks back, one doesn't find humanity in its present soul-spiritual constitution, but in the world of divine-spiritual beings in whom man resided in a seminal state. These are the Primal Forces (archai).' (GA 26, around New Year 1925, part 1)

During the arupa period, the seeds of the animals still lived as a condition of consciousness in the archangels; the seeds of the plants, as conditions of consciousness of the angels; and the minerals, as thought-seeds in man and simultaneously as thoughts in the consciousness of the Spirits of Form. During the rupa stage, which followed arupa, the animals then separated out as independent thought-beings from the consciousness of the archangels; likewise, during the subsequent astral phase, the plants separated as independent astral beings from the consciousness of the angels; and finally, at the beginning of the physical condition of form, the minerals separated out from the consciousness of man as independent etheric formations which only later condensed to physical form. (GA 11, 'The Life of the Earth', not quoted) Thus the archai, archangels, and angels are connected with the essential being of man, animal, and plant; and man with the minerals.

The beings of the minerals were thus released to an existence of their own from the consciousness of man, whereas the first elementary kingdom, which forms the minerals' physical body, was released from the consciousness of the archai. The being of the plants arose from the consciousness of the angels, whereas the second elementary kingdom, which shapes their etheric body, arose from the consciousness of the archangels. And the being of animals, before they appeared as separate beings, lived in the consciousness of the archangels, whereas the third elementary kingdom, which shapes their astral body, arose in the consciousness of the angels. The beings of humanity rested as seeds in the consciousness of the archai, but the elementary kingdom that shapes their thought-body is their own kingdom.

10.2 The future development of the higher members-of-being

Once the human being has attained self-consciousness in his Ego, there opens up for him the potential and task, out of the Ego's own power, to elaborate and make his own the rudiments of his higher members-of-being. By way of preparation the human being has already worked more or less unconsciously on his lower members. So far he has developed the sentient-soul in the astral body as a faint preliminary stage of spirit-self; he has developed the intellectual or mind-soul in the etheric body as a preliminary stage of life-spirit; and finally the consciousness-soul in the physical body as a preliminary stage of spirit-man. These three soul members at first comprise modifications or parts of the astral body. (GA 121, 9 June 1910, not quoted) 'The human Ego initially lives its inner life predominantly in these three members, and, during our fifth post-Atlantean cultural epoch, it will become and live at its most inward in the consciousness-soul, because in the consciousness-soul the pure Ego can express itself completely unhindered, so to speak, by the other members.' (GA 130, 9 January 1912)

Today the physical, etheric, and astral bodies are still worked on by the extra-human elementary kingdoms. By the Ego gaining mastery over the formative thought-forces of these elementary kingdoms, it can free its lower members from all foreign influences. Thus in the future the Ego will build these lower members out of its own power using the spiritual thought-seed forces of higher Devachan, which also comprise the rudiments of the higher members. The lower members will thus gradually dovetail into the nascent rudiments of the higher ones, 'filling out' as it were the as yet empty forms of the higher members; and the place of the divine powers that at present still look after these higher members will be taken by the human Ego itself.

The first goal for man is to purify his drives, desires, passions, and wishes and thereby gain power over his astral body. By this process he will increasingly learn how to manage the laws and formative forces of the spirit realm with which the animal kingdom is still active as the third elementary kingdom in his astral body. This development of spirit-self has already begun. A beginning of spirit-self exists in everyone, and the human astral body thus consists of a part already transformed and a part not yet governed by the human being. 'As much of what originally lived in man's astral body, and has been brought under the mastery of his Ego, we call spirit-self.' (GA 99, 25 May 1907) The part of the human astral body that is not yet transformed is looked after by our guiding angel.

We are at present living in the fifth post-Atlantean cultural epoch. In the next, the sixth epoch, the further development of spirit-self, initially at the soul level, will reach a certain climax.

> This will be a Manas culture when the sources of truth will be felt more and more in the now-strong individuality, in the personal aspect of people, and when simultaneously what is experienced as high truth will be the same for everyone, like mathematical truths. . . . Thus, during the course of the sixth cultural epoch when spirit-self will enter human beings, there will indeed be a spiritual sun to which all people will incline and in which they will all be in agreement. (GA 103, 30 May 1908)

The full development of spirit-self, however, will only take place with the next embodiment of the earth, the Jupiter condition. 'This astral body actually becomes a new member-of-being in man when he has given himself, as an astral being, a sculptural form.' (GA 103, 30 May 1908) Man will then give himself this sculptural form using the same formative forces of thought—namely the seed-thoughts of the soul level in the fifth region of spirit land—with which, during the Moon period when he himself was in the third elementary kingdom, his astral body was first established without his conscious participation. The Ego will then be able to separate itself from its physical and etheric bodies and be able to direct these from outside. (GA 121, 7 June 1910, not quoted)

For people of our times the process of transforming the etheric body to *life-spirit* takes place for the most part unconsciously. It is brought about by gaining mastery over habits and temperament, through art, and above all through religious impulses. (GA 97, 17 March 1907, not quoted) Thus we can already work unconsciously on transforming our etheric body to life-spirit by looking at works of art, and by devotional contemplation and prayer, where regular repetition is particularly important. Conscious development of life-spirit will begin during the seventh cultural epoch. It will only be completed in the future Venus existence; then the individual will feel himself entirely as a member of humanity. The etheric body was established during the Sun period using seed-thoughts of the sixth region of the spiritual realm, with which primal humanity was connected at that time as the second elementary kingdom. At the present time it is the primal beings of the plant kingdom that work with these life forces on the human etheric body. When the Ego gains full mastery over the etheric body, it will shape its etheric body using these formative thought forces itself. As long as this has not yet occurred, the human etheric body is taken care of by the archangelic folk spirits.

The thought-seed forces for spiritualizing the physical body are to be found in the highest region of spirit land. It was with these forces that the human physical body was first established on Old Saturn, when primal humanity, with these seed-thoughts, constituted the first elementary kingdom. Today it is the primal beings of the minerals that work with these forces on the human physical body. But these thought-seed forces must also be absorbed into his being by man. This begins with mastery of the breath. *Atma* or *atman* means 'to breathe' {'to breathe' in German is '*atmen*'}. When we have transformed our physical body to spirit-man, which will not occur until Vulcan, then human beings will attain 'the ability to look into themselves so that the movements of the nerve strands, pulse beats, currents of breath, all become clear, so that the human being can work into these consciously'. (GA97, 17 March 1907)

> When we reach that stage of development, it is then possible that not a single particle in our body moves without our willing it.... The transformation of the physical body goes hand in hand with gaining power over the forces that flow throughout the whole cosmos. (GA 100, 18 June 1907)

> When the time comes that the human being can lift his consciousness [into the higher sections of the mental plane], then he prepares his physical body himself out of the materials of the world. (GA 93a, 28 September 1905)

At present it is the archai who, following the ideal form created by the Spirits of Form, fashion the human physical body. The lower human members are thus organized by the beings of the third hierarchy, just as the rudiments of our higher members are organized by the beings of the second hierarchy.

The spiritualization of the lower members-of-being is thus a process whereby these members, bestowed on the Ego by the gods and consisting of substances of the lower worlds, are purified of these substances by the Ego, and permeated by it with spiritual thought-seed forces. The members having been fully developed, and now belonging completely to the Ego, are then integrated once more by the Ego into the higher regions of spirit land, from where once upon a time they were first laid down in rudimentary form.

The foundations for the transformation of the lower members-of-being are created by man during earthly life, whereas the development of the higher members takes place in Devachan during the intermediary state between death and a new birth. For it is here that the Ego unites itself with its higher members, which are still borne by divine forces, and integrates into them the fruits of its past life.

> When the human being passes over after death into the Sun sphere, his lowest member is actually the Ego, and the next lowest structure is spirit-self, then life-spirit, then spirit-man—those structures which will be present physically only in later periods of earth's development, but which the human being develops in spiritual circumstances between death and a new birth.... Just as, when he comes down to birth, he receives his physical and etheric bodies, so he receives his life-spirit and spirit-man when he passes through the portal of death, as that with which he is then clothed. (GA 208, 21 October 1921)

> When [after death, the human being] has passed through the soul world, he meets a world containing spiritual things.... But the human being still makes a distinction between what belongs to his Ego and what is the environment of the Ego, what comprises its spiritual surroundings.... The entire surroundings of the human being are filled with spiritual beings that are of the same kind as his Ego, for only an Ego has access to another Ego.... But the human being brings something with him into this world which is not surroundings: it is what the Ego has experienced in the world of the senses.... It is the spiritual harvest of life, the fruit of life. This harvest is of a spiritual nature. It contains everything of a spiritual nature that revealed itself through the senses. But without life in the sense world this could not have come about. After death the Ego feels this spiritual fruit from the sense world to be its own, its inner world. (GA 13, 'Sleep and Death')

When the human being enters Devachan after death, he:

> no longer has in his possession what the gods had worked into his etheric and astral body. However, what he himself has attained through work during many lives now belongs to him; it is his own also in Devachan. What human beings do in the physical world serves to make them more and more conscious in Devachan.... Hence the infinite importance of life on the physical plane. For human evolution there is no other way to awaken the organs for Devachan than by spiritual activity on the physical plane.... This is why the devachanic world is called the world of effects, and the physical world, the world of causes. The human being could never form his higher organs except by seeking the cause for these organs on the physical plane. It is for this

purpose that humanity is placed on the physical plane. (GA 93a, 9 October 1905)

[In Devachan] you have before you in vast, mighty pictures, everything that flowed into physical life.... And human beings in Devachan constantly absorb something from the life of their environment, and construct for themselves a kind of spirit-organism out of the elements of this environment. They continuously feel themselves to be beings in a state of becoming, for whom, member by member, a spiritual organism arises. (GA 109, 6 June 1909)

While human beings in the spirit realm shape the organs of their devachanic members-of-being, they imprint the originally formless thought-seed substance of the arupa plane into their own forms:

To the extent that one ploughs through the physical plane and understands it, one attains the ability to carry up to the arupa plane the things one has learnt in the physical world. In itself the arupa plane is formless; but it gets forms through human life. Human beings gather lessons on the physical plane and carry them into arupa. This is why in Greek esotericism the soul was called a bee, the arupa plane a hive, and the physical world a flower meadow. (GA 93a, 6 October 1905)

At the end of our cycle of creation, on Vulcan, the human members-of-being will be so spiritualized that they will exist on the arupa plane purely as thought-seeds, but ones that contain all the forces for new formations, like the thought-seeds that made possible the formation of the human members-of-being at the beginning of evolution on Saturn.

Similarly to the way the octave represents a repetition as it were of the first note, just at a higher level, so is the Vulcan condition a repetition of the Saturn condition, only at a higher level of development. The whole cosmos has evolved from spirit, and with the Vulcan condition everything will have evolved back to spirit, just at a higher and more diverse level of development. From one spirituality infinitely many spirit-humans have arisen. (GA 100, 23 June 1907)

In the higher spirit realms the unity of all being reigns supreme; thus atma, the substance of spirit-man, is also an undifferentiated whole to begin with, from which the primal beings appropriate, as it were, a part for themselves.

The higher bodies flow into one another; in truth, for example, there is one atma for all humanity, like a common atmosphere. However, the

> atma of individual people is to be understood as everyone cutting a piece for himself out of the common atma, so that cuts, as it were, are made into it. (GA 93a, 9 October 1905)

By appropriating a piece of common atma for himself, and by developing himself to a self-conscious and independent Ego, the human being has released himself as a separate being from the general spirit-organism, of which he was originally an unconscious and dependent member. Humanity must relinquish this separateness by selflessly integrating itself once more into the spirit-organism.

> We have to overcome this separation. We do this by making human relationships of a purely soul nature. By doing this we 'suspend the separateness' and recognize the unity of atma in everything. By making human connections, I awaken a sympathy in myself, I take on the work of integrating myself with the cosmic plan.... In the relationship of soul to soul we have a powerful means of developing devachanic organs. What people develop at present by way of soul capacity—for example, in pure soul friendship—is wisdom in Devachan.... By being engaged with things at a purely soul level, the human being grows eyes for Devachan.... There is no better preparation than a soul relationship with people, a soul relationship that originally had no natural basis. (GA 93a, 9 October 1905)

> Thus, by establishing soul connections here {on earth}, we work on the form that Devachan contains. All, all of us have worked in this way by establishing bonds of love; in doing this we have created something that has significance not only for the earth but which shapes conditions in Devachan. We could say: what happens here through love, through friendship, through heartfelt mutual understanding—these are building blocks that build temples above in the spiritual region. And for people who are permeated by the certainty of this, it has to be an uplifting feeling to know that when they create bonds here from soul to soul, this is the foundation of an eternal process of becoming. (GA 99, 29 May 1907)

There is also another way for the human being to give up his separateness on the physical plane:

> by merging with the surrounding world, with the not-I. Only the first beginnings exist of a mental life in the physical world. These beginnings are there, for example, when one looks at a work of art with a pure contemplation, without any wish to own it. Regarding a work of

> art is an important act of soul when, forgetting oneself, one works at it purely as a mental task. [One must] learn to 'un-self' one's wishes on the physical plane. (GA 93a, 6 October 1905)

As a self-conscious, independent, but selfless being, man will integrate himself again with the spiritual cosmos and carry the fruits of his evolution into the thought-seed substance, the primal substance, of the arupa world. By doing so he will imprint into this primal substance the forces of his being just as, at the beginning of Saturn's evolution, it was permeated by the forces of Throne-being. Man will have matured in turn to the point of 'The Great Sacrifice', through which he will be able to contribute 'to further work on the higher worlds'. (GA 10, not quoted) The fact that he will be able to do this, that by forming his higher members-of-being himself he will be able to contribute to the progress of cosmic existence—all this is possible by virtue of the appearance of Christ on earth.

> What we will still develop during the remainder of earth's evolution—a certain deepening and strengthening of the Ego—we will do thanks to the earth and its forces. But we have to say that if we wanted to attribute our human being purely to the earth and its forces, then we could never develop a spirit-man, a life-spirit, or a spirit-self. For these are things the earth cannot give. It can only stimulate us to develop the Ego.... In order to become a complete human being, to unfold in ourselves everything that we have to develop in the future as spirit-self, life-spirit, and spirit-man, ... we have to look away from the earth to what has come into it from extraterrestrial levels. We have to look to Christ and say: Christ brought into the earth the non-earthly forces which can stimulate us to develop what the earth itself could never stimulate.... We need to learn to recognize Christ as the one who has saved our humanity. (GA 197, 22 November 1920)

Cyclical evolution thus turns full circle as follows. During the Saturn, Sun, and Moon phases two kinds of human origin arise: a lower man consisting of physical, etheric and astral body, and a higher man, in rudimentary form, consisting of spirit-self, life-spirit, and spirit-man. During earth evolution these two sources are united by the I. Earth evolution is thus the turning-point. Primal human beings with the dullest of consciousnesses came forth from the highest region of spirit land. As fully developed spirit beings with the brightest consciousness they will, through the power of the Christ impulse, return as spirit-humans at the end of our cycle of creation, the Vulcan phase, to the highest region. And the energies of thought-seed substance in the higher regions of spirit land, the forces of being of high divine-spiritual powers who have served primal humanity on its whole evolutionary path as cosmic thought-forces of form, will then be replaced by the 'being-forces' of humanity itself.

The primal human beings or monads themselves, however, will then separate from the seed substance of the higher spirit region in order 'to enter pure Purusha as free souls'. (GA 142, 29 December 1912) The monads will then be 'pure inner being', just as the Spirits of Will were at the beginning of Saturn evolution, 'spiritual being that is complete in itself and needs no external being to become conscious of itself'. (GA 13, 'World Evolution and Man', section on 'Saturn Evolution')

11. The Shaping of the Human Members-of-Being by the Elementary Kingdoms

11.1 The Creation of the lower members-of-being

The passage of the primal beings or life kernels through the elementary kingdoms and the formation of the lower human members-of-being was discussed from different angles in the preceding chapters. Below we will look at them briefly again with reference to what has been said about the first rudiments and development of the higher members.

Everything that is to arise in the three worlds has its origin in the higher regions of spirit land, in arupa, and has to be laid down and given its characteristics by the thought-seed forces there. Then, in the lower regions of spirit land, in the rupa world, it gets pre-figured as a thought archetype from which in the astral, etheric, and physical worlds, using the substances of those worlds, images or reflections are shaped. Thus, initiated by the sacrifice of the Thrones, Saturn evolution began with the first condition of Form of the first Life Stage on the arupa plane. Everything that in due course was to develop during the Saturn phase to the point of warmth-formations—the first rudiments of the human physical body—was still present as thought-seed substance into which the Thrones had poured the spiritualized forces of their physical body.

It was into this, the highest region of the spirit realm, that the life kernels of the primal beings of humanity were placed at the beginning of Saturn evolution, presumably also by the Thrones. The life kernels united with the formative seeds of the physical level, thus giving rise to the first elementary kingdom of Saturn. The life kernels imprinted the as yet indefinite thought-seed substance of the physical with their own urge to become—received by them as a predisposition from their divine origin—and formed thereby, in the lowest region of spirit land, the archetype of their physical body. Subsequently, at the physical Stage of Form, this then condensed to a physical warmth body. On Saturn, as also during the following embodiments of the earth, this physical body was a form body, the phantom, which was filled out with the corresponding physical materiality of each phase: with warmth substance on Saturn; with warmth and airy substance on Old Sun; with warmth, airy, and watery substance on Moon; and with solid, earthy substance on Earth. Up to the Lemurian period of earth's evolution the physical substance filling the phantom was still in an elemental condition which then, by absorbing mineral substance, condensed to its present, externally perceptible form.

After Saturn, during the Sun period, primal humanity descended to the second highest region of spirit land, to the region of {thought-}seeds of life. The Spirits of Wisdom had poured their life-spirit energies into this region, providing the thought-seeds there with the forces to fashion etheric bodies as the bearers of life. By uniting with these seminal life forces, the primal beings of humanity comprised the second elementary kingdom of the Sun period, and as such created an archetype of the etheric body in the second lowest region. The human etheric body, as the second member-of-being, arose as a living reflection of this archetype and permeated the physical body with forces of life and growth. During the Sun period, the human life kernels no longer worked directly as formative forces on the human physical body. This was done now by the life kernels of the new line of evolution, the animal kingdom, which, comprising the first elementary kingdom, forms its own and man's physical body from the highest realm of spirit regions.

During the Moon period, the Spirits of Movement united the forces of their spirit-self with the thought-seed substances of the fifth region of spirit land, the soul region, into which the human life kernels now also descend as the third elementary kingdom. The human life kernels, using the soul-related seed forces of the third region, fashion a thought-archetype of soul, the 'true astral body', the 'true self'. As a reflection of this on the astral plane, the astral body arises as the third human member-of-being, which imbues the physical-etheric body with sensation and consciousness. During Old Moon the formative forces of the animals, now risen to the second elementary kingdom, worked on both the human and animal etheric body. The physical body of both is worked on by the newly arrived life kernels of the plant kingdom, comprising the first elementary kingdom, which also form their own physical moon-body.

During the earth's evolution, the human life kernels united with the thought-seed substance of the spiritual level in the fourth region of spirit land, into which the Spirits of Form had poured the forces of their 'Egohood'. Using these seed forces, the human life kernels created in the same region the archetype of their thought-body, their Ego-member. Through this the {mental and} spirit being of man can manifest itself within the body of senses and become aware of itself through thinking. The primal beings, which prior to this had been bound to a group soul, now individualize into separate human spirits. 'The spirit has become the inner being of man. The form which the formless spirit-being in man takes, is thought.' (GA 9, *The Three Worlds V*) The life kernels of the animal kingdom now work as third elementary kingdom in the astral body of man and animal. The life kernels of the plant kingdom work as second elementary kingdom in the etheric body of man, animal, and plant. Today the first elementary kingdom is comprised of the life kernels of the minerals which work on the physical body of man, animal, and plant, as well as on their own physical body.

Just as the 'substance' aspect of the physical body became ever more complex by the gradual addition, to the original warmth substance, of the airy and watery elements, so was this also the case with the etheric and astral body. During Old Sun, the human etheric body consisted of the warmth-ether brought over from Saturn, and light-ether. Tone-ether was added during the Moon period, and life-ether during the earth phase. The human astral body also consists of two different astralities: a lower one which had its origin on Old Moon, and a higher one that first entered human nature during the Earth period.

Each planetary existence saw the introduction into evolution of a new species of being within the three worlds: the primal human beings on Saturn; the animals on Sun; the plants on Moon; and the minerals on earth. We can assume that future embodiments of the earth will see the introduction of yet other species of being whose life kernels are still resting in the lap of the Godhead beyond our three worlds. Thus there arises wave after wave of being from the divine ground of all existence, in incalculable number and variety.

11.2 Laying down the rudiments for the higher members of the human being

The first rudiments of the higher members-of-being—spirit-self (manas), life-spirit (buddhi), and spirit-man (atma)—also arose, like the lower members, in connection with the passage of primal human beings or life kernels through the elementary kingdoms. These higher members consist of the formless thought-seed substances of the three upper regions of spirit land, with which the rudiments of the lower members-of-being were also first established. The higher principles will one day be nothing less than the lower members re-spiritualized—that is, transformed back into thought-seed substance once again—by the work of the Ego. So, for example, 'this manas is the result of a transformation of the astral body by the Ego. In "substance" it is the same as the astral body; it is just a different arrangement of what the astral body was originally, which has been transformed into spirit-self.' (GA 99, 25 May 1907)

The rudiments of the lower members-of-being were bestowed on man by divine-spiritual beings using the thought-seed forces of the elementary kingdoms comprised of the human life kernels. On the other hand, the human life kernels created the rudiments of the higher members themselves once they had reached a certain level of consciousness, albeit a very dim one. Thus the first rudiment of the human physical body arose during the first Life Stage of Saturn's evolution, whereas the rudiment of spirit-man arose only in the last, the seventh, Life Stage. For, according to the law of cyclical development, the way evolution passes through the Life Stages is such that in the middle of a planetary development a turning back takes place, and descent is succeeded by re-ascent to the stages at the outset. The rudiment of spirit-man was thus first laid down once Saturn's evolution had returned back to the arupa condition—the condition from which the physical body had also originated.

> Around the middle of the seventh Saturn cycle . . . man has come to the point where he can work unconsciously on his own material body. Through this activity he creates, in the complete dullness of Saturn existence, the first seminal rudiment of the actual 'spirit-self'. . . . In itself it [atma] would at this stage be completely dull and unconscious. But just as the Seraphim and Cherubim of their own free will revealed themselves in the two previous stages of human development, so it is the Thrones who do so now—those beings who, at the very beginning of Saturn's evolution, rayed out the human body from their own being. The seed of 'spirit-man' [atma] is completely permeated by the power of these Spirits of Will, and retains this power through all subsequent stages of development. (GA 11, 'The Life of Saturn')

> Man had no independent existence on Saturn; but higher beings permeated him with their etheric body, astral body, Ego, and so on. (GA 104, 27 June 1908)

In *Occult Science* the establishing of the rudiment of spirit-man is mentioned only briefly. Towards the end of Saturn's evolution the human phantoms are permeated by the Spirits of Will.

> The result of this is that the human phantom appears with the simplest, dullest form of consciousness. We must picture this form of consciousness as being lower than that of dreamless sleep. . . . It brings the inner being into harmony with the external physical world. On Saturn it is the Spirits of Will who regulate this harmony. . . . And this process gives the first seed for what is still seminal in man today: spirit-man [atma]. (GA 13, 'World Development and Man', section of Saturn evolution)

The laying down of the rudiment for spirit-man occurs through the life kernels separating out and uniting themselves with parts of the undifferentiated thought-seed substance of the highest region of spirit land, with which they are connected. 'The higher bodies flow into one another; for example, in truth there is one atma for the whole of humanity, like a common atmosphere. However, the atma of an individual can be understood as though everyone cuts a piece for himself out of the common atma, so that cuts, as it were, are made in it.' (GA 93a, 9 October 1905)

The first rudiment of the second highest human member-of-being, of *life-spirit*, arose during Old Sun in the sixth region of spirit land, into which the Spirits of Wisdom had poured, as the substance of their own being, the forces of their spiritualized etheric body. Again it was the primal human beings themselves who—now as second elementary kingdom—created from these seed-forces of life the seminal rudiment of their own life-spirit, and were aided in this by the Cherubim.

> From the middle of the sixth Sun cycle onwards, man has reached the point of being able to work unconsciously on his physical body.... By this activity he creates in dullness {of consciousness} the seminal rudiment of living spirit-being we call 'life-spirit' [buddhi].... Just as from the seventh Saturn cycle onwards the Thrones, of their own free will, poured their energy into the rudiment of spirit-man that had been formed there, so the Cherubim now pour out their wisdom which is retained in the life-spirit of human beings through all subsequent stages of development. From the middle of the seventh Sun cycle onwards, the seed of spirit-man [atma], that was first laid down on Saturn, re-emerges. It connects with life-spirit [buddhi], giving rise to the life-imbued monad [atma-buddhi]. (GA 11, 'The Life of the Sun')

Here again, in accord with cyclical development, the laying down of the rudiment of life-spirit occurred only once the evolution of Old Sun had reascended into the sixth region of spirit land. And the union of the seed of life-spirit with the seed of spirit-man took place only in the seventh region.

The laying down of the rudiment of *spirit-self* also only took place in the fifth cycle of Old Moon when primal humanity, as the third elementary kingdom and in the fifth region of the spiritual realm, had united with the thought-seed substance of soul given by the Spirits of Movement. The primal human beings were helped in this by the Seraphim.

> In the middle of the fifth Moon cycle, [man] reached the point of being able to act unconsciously on his physical body. In doing so he creates in the dullness of his consciousness the seminal rudiment of what we call 'spirit-self' [manas]. . . . Just as the Thrones or Spirits of Will permeated spirit-man on Saturn, and the Cherubim permeated life-spirit on Old Sun, so the Seraphim do the same now for spirit-self. They permeate and thereby implant in it a capacity which in later stages of development—on earth—will become the ability to form mental pictures through which man as a thinking being can come into relationship with the world around him. [From the middle of the sixth and seventh Moon cycle onwards life-spirit and spirit-man re-emerge respectively], 'and unite with spirit-self, so that by the end of the whole cosmic Moon period, the "higher man" is prepared'. (GA 11, 'Life on Moon')

In the middle of the earth period, in the physical Stage of Form of the fourth Life Stage, the union took place *in the Ego* of the lower members-of-being with the rudiments of the higher members.

Thus the rudiments were established as follows:

Physical body	in 1st Saturn cycle	— Spirit-man	in 7th Saturn cycle
Etheric body	in 2nd Sun cycle	— Life-spirit	in 6th Sun cycle
Astral body	in 3rd Moon cycle	— Spirit-self	in 5th Moon cycle
	the Ego in 4th Earth cycle		

This creation sequence of our members-of-being shows clearly the harmony in the laws at work in the cosmic plan and its unfolding, which can only fill us with wonder and reverence. As a gift from the Spirits of Form, the Ego came from below, as it were, to the already-present three lower members. 'When the consciousness-soul was sufficiently advanced that during life on earth it could fashion for itself a body that was suitable for it, the Spirits of Form bestowed on it a spark from their fire. The Ego was ignited in it.' (GA 13, 'Cosmic Evolution and Man,' the section on Earth evolution) From the other side, the sequence of higher principles in their rudimentary form was continued from above by the 'soul as inner being', the image of the 'true I'. The union of the lower and higher members occurred during the earth's Lemurian period, after the separation from the earth of the sun and moon.

> Due to this progress in the earth's development, it became possible to integrate into the threefold human nature, as it was after Moon, the fourth member, the Ego. . . . But this was also the time when a higher principle was integrated into the fourfold being of humanity: the soul as inner being. (GA 11, 'Fourfold Man on Earth')

The Ego or I, the soul as inner being, was also initially given to humanity only in rudimentary form, which it was to develop fully in the course of earth evolution, and likewise with the other higher members in the subsequent embodiments of the earth.

Humanity's lower members were bestowed on it in descending order, as it were, by the Thrones, Spirits of Wisdom, Spirits of Movement, and Spirits of Form. With the rudiments of the higher members help was given, in ascending order, by the Thrones, Cherubim, and Seraphim. We would therefore expect that, with the integration of the Ego as inner being into human nature, help was given by the power of a being extending beyond the Seraphim. This high being, who permeates the Ego with its forces, is the Christ being. 'The highest spirit, who is united with the sun and sent down the Egos to the earth, is called in esoteric teachings, Christ. However, the Egos as parts of the Sun Logos streamed only gradually into the forms {on earth}. (GA 100, 18 November 1907)

Primal humanity was able, in its dim consciousness, to form the rudiments of its higher principles with help from higher powers because each principle was fashioned from the seed-thoughts with which the primal beings, as elementary kingdoms, were connected. By contrast, the rudiments of the lower members-of-being, consisting of 'denser' substances, had to be given by the gods because the primal beings were not yet able to work on these substances themselves. They will only become able to do this in later embodiments of the earth. It is striking, however, that the creation of the rudiments of the higher members by the primal beings themselves is always connected by Rudolf Steiner with their own work on their physical body. Consciousness awakens by means of the physical; and this applies also to the dim forms of consciousness in the early stages of evolution. The fashioning of the seeds for the higher members by the primal beings themselves always occurred when, guided by higher beings, they worked actively on their physical body, and were able through this to bring their inner aspect into relationship with their physical surroundings. Initially this harmony with the external environment was still regulated by higher beings—thus, on Saturn, by the Thrones. Only during earth evolution did the human being become able to experience consciously, in the Ego, the things that exist and are happening in his environment, and thereby come to full self-consciousness.

Even though the human being on Saturn consisted as yet only of a physical body, nevertheless the forces of the higher members-of-being were already active in it. For a being can only exist in a physical body if the forces of the other members are exerting an influence on it. As long as these are not yet present, their forces have to be provided for human beings by divine-spiritual beings out of the general cosmos. Even the rudiments of higher members that are permeated by the beings of the first hierarchy are already at work in the human being.

> Christian esotericism rightly says that in the human physical body there is already that which will be there one day when man stands at the pinnacle of his development, but it is divine atma, divine-spiritual being. And buddhi is already in the etheric body, but it is divine life-spirit ... [And in the part of the astral body not yet governed by the human being] there is spirit-self, but divine spirit-self. (GA 103, 19 May 1908)

From the earliest times of earth evolution the rudiments of the higher human members-of-being, the 'spiritual man', were taken care of by the beings of the first hierarchy, with whose help they first arose. The care of these higher members was transferred, in the second half of the third Life Stage of earth development, to the beings of the second hierarchy. 'The Thrones, Cherubim, and Seraphim rise to higher spheres, and spiritual man now is supported by the Spirits of Wisdom, of Movement, and of Form. These are now united with spirit-self, life-spirit, and spirit-man.' (GA 11, 'The Life of the Earth')

12. The passage of the earth through the elementary kingdoms and the Stages of Form

In each Life Stage, the evolution of beings takes place through seven Stages of Form. At the beginning of the Life Stage, the beings exist as formless thought-seeds on the arupa plane. They then descend to the rupa plane where they create thought-archetypes from the thought-seed forces. Descending further to the astral plane, the beings clothe themselves, as it were, in soul replicas of the archetypes, formed of astral substance. Finally, they descend to the physical plane to appear in physical form. Having completed this, the beings move once again—but now in a different, more highly developed state—into the astral condition; then into the condition of thought-archetypes; and finally into the condition of thought-seed beings.

According to a cosmic law, when something new is to arise in world evolution there must first be a brief repetition of the old, adapting it to the new conditions. Thus at the beginning of its present evolution, the earth with all its creatures first passed briefly through conditions of Old Saturn, Sun, and Moon. To begin with there arose again a mighty body of warmth or fire in which the same processes—but at a higher level—took place as during the Saturn period. The Sun and Moon evolutions were then repeated in the same way. This repetition of the three preceding planetary conditions signified for the earth its *passage through the elementary kingdoms*, that is, through the first three Life Stages. In *Occult Science* it is described as follows:

> The human being had first to be got ready to receive what was to be given him. He had integrated the physical, etheric, and astral body into his being during the Saturn, Sun, and Moon evolutions.... In order to develop a higher stage of consciousness, these {bodies} had first to undergo a preparation. This happened in three preliminary stages.
>
> During the first stage, the physical body was refined to a point where it could receive the necessary restructuring that could enable it to become the foundation for an objective consciousness. We can call this preliminary stage of earth's evolution a repetition of the Saturn period at a higher level. For, during this stage, only the physical body is worked on by higher beings, as was the case during Saturn. Once the physical body is sufficiently advanced in its development, all the beings

must first pass over into a higher form of existence before the life-body can advance. The physical body must be re-cast, as it were, in order to be able in its further development to absorb the life-body, which is also now more highly formed.

After this intermediary period in a higher form of existence, a repetition of the Sun evolution commences, at a higher level, to develop the life-body. And something similar, again after an intermediary period, occurs for the astral body in a repetition of Moon evolution. (GA 13, 'World Development and Man')

The repetition of the Saturn period represents the passage of earth evolution through the first elementary kingdom; that of Sun, the passage through the second elementary kingdom; and that of the Moon period, the passage through the third elementary kingdom. After another spiritualization of all beings (pralaya), the fourth Life Stage begins—the mineral kingdom—and thereby earth evolution proper, which was to bring to man a new element and fourth member of his being: the Ego. Development during this period also followed a course from the arupa level to the rupa and astral levels, and to the physical Stage of Form, in which the earth and its beings find themselves at present.

Rudolf Steiner refers to this passage of the earth through the three elementary kingdoms in a lecture in 1905. When the earth re-emerges from pralaya after the Old Moon evolution, to begin with it enters the *first elementary kingdom.*

Man was in the first Round [Life Stage] in the first elementary kingdom. When he became physical, he was initially in the first elementary kingdom. It was in the physical Globe [Stage of Form] of the first Round that the thought-seed became physical. The earth consisted at that time of myriads of physical spheres, so small that one would not have been able to see them. They were myriads of points of energy. These energy points gradually condensed; there was no distinction between them at that time. The condensed elementary kingdom was indeed physical. If we think of man as a mere thought-being, we can easily walk through such a being. Once he is physical, we can't walk through him even if we can't see him. The physical points of energy became astral again and then passed over into the subsequent Round. (GA 93a, 27 October 1905)

We can understand this statement if we consider that, during the whole of this first Round, everything belonging to the earth and which was later to evolve on it, only existed in a seminal state, and did not leave the highest spiritual, the arupa, condition. The earth consisted at that time of myriads of thought-seed points without form. When these are described in the quote above as spheres, we are talking here of spheres without content; at the same time they are also called points of energy. During this first Life Stage, the earth—consisting of these thought-seed points that represent, as it were, the intentions and goals for cosmic creation still resting in the consciousness of the creator powers—developed through the seven Stages of Form. These thought-seeds of the gods—which nonetheless were realities, living thought-entities—contained the blueprint for the human physical body, but in seed form, in the way this had been prepared by the evolutions of Saturn, Sun, and Moon. In this blueprint of the human physical form was also contained in seminal condition everything that, during the further course of evolution, was extruded, separated out as the physical forms of the plant and animal.

Naturally it is difficult to get a proper idea of these thought-seed points, particularly when it is also said that they condense to the point of physicality and are therefore impenetrable. And yet, in the first Life Stage, this was the case as the earth passed through this Round's physical Stage of Form. Still today the seer finds physical things in elementary existence without materiality, that show themselves as 'solid' and impenetrable even though they are supersensory and externally imperceptible. (GA 119, 26 March 1910, not quoted)

Development in the *second elementary kingdom* also still took place within the thought-world of the gods, but now at the rupa level in the form of shaped thoughts, as thought images. For, after everything in this second Round had again emerged from the arupa world of formless thought-seed entities, the thought-seed points structure themselves in the second Stage of Form at the rupa level into thought-forms, into archetypes. The thought-forms then passed as these archetypes through the other Stages of Form. 'In the second Round, the whole earth consisted of myriads of forms. The world was a beautifully formed sphere in which everything that later emerged already existed as prototype. It was a prophetic elaboration of everything that emerged in the other kingdoms. On earth, colours and forms were pre-images of present humanity.' (GA 93a, 27 October 1905)

We should not imagine these forms and colours of the second elementary kingdom, of the second Round, as being any more physical or sense-perceptible than the energy points of the first elementary kingdom. These thought forms become impenetrable again at the physical Stage of Form. Just as, during the passage of the earth through the first elementary kingdom, the physical body was transformed for further development, so the same happens now, in the second elementary kingdom, for the etheric body.

In the *third elementary kingdom*, during the third Life Stage, evolution descended a stage lower to the astral plane. At the astral level, the thought forms of the rupa plane become astral structures by clothing themselves with astral material, so to speak. The earth beings then passed over as these astral structures to the physical Stage of Form, became impenetrable once more, but without becoming externally visible. The human physical body was at that time 'an entity with physical laws in soul form. The case was similar for the life-body.' (GA 13) The blueprint of the astral body was now added to those of the physical and etheric bodies.

When, through recapitulation of the three previous embodiments of the earth, the lower human members-of-being had been prepared to receive the Ego, the initial structure for this could be integrated into the human being during the following, the mineral, Life Stage.

Rudolf Steiner goes into more detail about the earth's course of development during the *fourth Life Stage*, the mineral kingdom, where he occasionally refers to the arupa condition as *akasha*, and the rupa condition as *ether*.

> With the transition from the third to the fourth Round, at the beginning of the fourth Round, all the beings which had arisen in the third Round appeared again in the akasha. While developing further out of the akasha, everything had to condense, had to take on a denser form. This occurred during the rupa phase of the earth. In occultism this more material form is called ... the ether. Everything is contained in this etheric earth only in thought. But behind this was still the akasha as a foundation. The ether condenses in turn to astral light. The third Globe [Stage of Form], the astral earth, lights up in the astral light; it radiates fully in purest astral light.... After this, the earth goes over into its present, physical, condition. (GA 93a, 5 October 1905)

Just as the physical has its origin on the arupa plane, so the etheric, the bearer of life, has its origin on the rupa plane. Hence the reference to the thought substance of the rupa plane as ether.

In *The Akashic Chronicle*, we find the following description of development to the point of the physical Stage of Form of the fourth Life Stage:

> To begin with everything that had existed before as beings in the mineral, plant, animal, and human kingdoms, has to separate off in a seed condition from the undifferentiated mass. Initially only our

human ancestors could appear as independent seeds once more.... All the other beings of the mineral, plant, and animal kingdoms continue to lead a non-independent existence. [For, at this stage, everything is still in the highly spiritual condition referred to as the 'formless' or arupa state. At our present stage of evolution, only the highest human thoughts—for example, mathematical concepts and ethical ideals—are woven of the substance which, at this level, is available to all beings.] Everything that is lower than this human ancestor can only appear as an activity in a higher being. Thus the animals exist as states of consciousness in the Spirits of Fire [archangels], the plants as states of consciousness in the Spirits of Twilight [angels], but the minerals have a double existence in thought: to begin with they exist as thought-seeds in the human ancestor, and then as thoughts in the consciousness of the Spirits of Form....

Now a kind of gradual densification takes place for everything. At the next stage, however, this 'density' is at first such as does not go beyond the density of thoughts. But at this level of density the animal beings, which had arisen in the previous cycle, were able to emerge. They separate off from the consciousness of the Fire Spirits and become independent thought-beings. We call this stage the 'formed' or rupa condition. The human being advances further in so far as his previously formless, independent thought-body is clothed by the Spirits of Form with a body of denser, formed thought-substance. The animals as independent beings consist here only of this substance.

A further densification takes place. The condition now reached can be compared to the one out of which the images of a dreamlike picture-consciousness are woven. We call this stage the astral stage. Our human ancestor progresses still further. In addition to the two other components, his being also receives a body consisting of astrality. So he now has an inner formless core of his being, a thought-body, and an astral body. The animals also receive an astral body; and the plants separate out as independent astral beings from the consciousness of the Spirits of Twilight.

Further progress in evolution consists in a continuation of the densification process to the condition we call physical. At first we are dealing with the subtlest of physical states, with that of the subtlest ether. Our human ancestor, in addition to his earlier components, receives the subtlest etheric body from the Spirits of Form. He now consists of a formless spirit-core, a formed thought-body, an astral body, and an etheric body. The animals have a formed thought-body, an astral body, and an etheric body. The plants have an astral and an

> etheric body. The minerals emerge now for the first time as independent etheric formations.... This covers the earth's course of formation up to the beginning of its physical condition. (GA 11, 'The Life of the Earth')

While the earth was passing through the astral Stage of Form, the etheric body (life-body), and the physical body that was still contained in the etheric body, were present in astral form. 'What makes the physical body physical is not its physical form but the fact that, although it possesses an astral form, it nevertheless contains physical laws.' (GA 13, 'World Evolution and Man')

The 'subtlest' ether of which the etheric body consisted at this time is elemental life-ether; it is from this that, since the beginning of the physical Stage of Form, the other types of elemental and physical ether have crystallized out. (GA 11, 'The Life of the Earth,' not quoted)

> One calls a condition through which the earth passes—beginning from the finest etheric material, condensing, and then returning to a condition of fine physical etheric material—a Stage of Form, or Globe. The physical Globe develops from an initial condition that is finer than the subtlest physical ether. The etheric arises from, and returns to, the astral. (GA 93a, 26 October 1905)

The phase of development just described refers to the beginning of the physical Stage of Form where everything was still in transition from the astral to the physical state. It was only at a later phase of this condensing process towards the physical that the physical-mineral body of all the earth beings separated from the etheric (elemental) body. The minerals too, which up to now had lived as thought-seeds in the consciousness of human beings, now also separate out from this as physical beings.

We find another description of development to the physical Stage of Form in the following:

> The fourth earthly Round began with the first arupic Globe emerging from the darkness of pralaya in which everything was dissolved. Everything that exists on the earth today was present at that time in formless thoughts. We can get the right idea about this if we restrict ourselves as much as possible to everything that was physical, and imagine it as thought-seeds. The forms weren't there yet, only the thoughts before they were structured. If we ask, 'So who had these thoughts?' the answer we get is that these were thoughts at that time of the spiritual beings who are connected with the earth; for example, Jehovah and his hosts were spiritual beings of this kind who filled

> everything around us on the earth. All things were present during the arupa Globe as thoughts of the gods. . . .
>
> The the arupa sphere condensed. Everything grew into thought-forms. The whole earth was filled with them, like looking into a large model composed of tiny crystals. During this rupa Globe, all the forms of human beings, animals, and plants were present like stereotypes; spiritual beings worked on these like a master craftsman on his models. They are put together from outside.
>
> The whole thing then goes over into astral matter; the astral Globe arises. (There are brief pralayas in between.) Here again it is divine powers, working externally, who pour out the astral matter and fill the forms with light and colour. At this stage all the astral form-structures of human beings, animals, and also the whole plant kingdom, find themselves in a great astral sea. This gradually condenses more and more, giving rise to the physical earth of the fourth Globe. (GA 93a, 28 October 1905)

It is only during this fourth Globe, in the physical Stage of Form, that the minerals appeared physically on earth.

During this passage of earth evolution through the astral Stage of Form, the physical and etheric bodies of human beings still had the same astral form as the astral body. About this *astral human being*, Steiner says:

> The astral human being, as it originally existed at that time, was a structure that was not like the present astral body but a far more encompassing entity. We can get an idea of this former astral body by imagining the earth at that time as astral, and composed of astral human beings. All the beings and forces of nature that are around us today were still within the human being at that time. Man lived dissolved in astral existence. All the plants, animals, and so on, the animal instincts and passions, also lived at that time in astral man. . . . The human astral body had within it at that time the entirety of all beings that are spread out over the earth. The astral earth was like a vast blackberry, composed of myriads of human astral bodies, and enclosed in a spiritual atmosphere in which devachanic beings lived. This astral sphere of air surrounding the earth at that time was composed of a somewhat thinner substance than the human astral bodies, and spiritual beings lived in it. . . . That was the condition of the earth at that time. . . .
>
> At first everything was astral, then physical material deposited itself around it. Through this, human structures became ever more suited to condensing and becoming an increasingly more complex and manifold organism. What became most dense was the physical body; less dense

was the etheric body, and the subtlest was the astral body.... By becoming increasingly subtle, the astral body came to approximate the subtle astral matter around it.

In the higher regions an opposite evolutionary process was taking place. In his descent from above, man had condensed. The monad had descended from above, from the highest Devachan regions, into the astral region. Here the two parts come to meet each other. On the one side the human being rises up to the astral body; on the other side the monad meets it in its descent into the astral world. This happened in the Lemurian period. Here the two were able to fructify each other. The monad clothed itself with devachanic material, then with astral air material, and then it meets astral material again from below. Thus the two astral materials fructify and merge into one another. The monad had within it what comes from above. As though into a bed, it embeds itself into the astral material. This is how the descent of the soul took place. (GA 93a, 24 October 1905) [The monad is the eternal spirit-core of the human being, his 'true I'.]

Thus there were two different streams of development which united and merged with one another during the Lemurian period of earth evolution. The spirit-being of man, the monad, descended from the arupa to the rupa and astral planes, clothing itself initially with thought-substance and then with finer astral substance (astral air material). At the same time, the monad had built up from below as it were its physical, etheric, and astral bodies out of denser material in preparation to receive the Ego. The union of the monad (the Ego) with its lower members-of-being could then take place in the Lemurian period.

In the present *physical Stage of Form* of the mineral Life Stage, all earthly beings emerge in physical form on the earth. After passing through this physical Stage of Form, evolution turns back once more, in a spiritualizing process, until it reaches the arupa plane. With reference to humanity's task at the physical Stage of Form, and its passage through the following Stages of Form, Rudolf Steiner discusses the following:

The earth is going through its fourth Round, and this is the mineral Round. The task of humanity during this time is to work on the mineral kingdom. It is already work on the mineral kingdom when someone takes a piece of flint and hammers it into a wedge-shape to use as a tool for other things. When he carries away rock and builds pyramids from its stone, when he makes metal tools, when he sends a network of electrical current over the earth—man is working on the mineral kingdom. He changes the earth completely into a work of art.

When an artist combines colour according to his manas, he is also working on the mineral kingdom. . . . [I]n the next race [Principal Age] it will be completely reworked so that in the end there will not be a single atom on the earth that has not been worked on by the human being. (GA 93a, 5 October 1905)

At present the human being is working on the mineral kingdom. When the time arrives in the future when he has finished working on and transforming the mineral kingdom, then this work on everything will be such that not a fragment of the mineral kingdom will still exist that the skill and artistry of the human being has not worked on. Then everything can change into myriads of astral forms. (GA 93a, 26 October 1905)

[Later] the whole mineral kingdom will be spiritualized by man. He ploughs it over with his mind. Everything that the human being does today . . . is a transformation of the mineral kingdom. When he removes a rock face in order to use the stone to build houses, or when he builds a cathedral—this is all skilful working of the mineral kingdom. In the fourth Round humanity has the skill to work on the mineral kingdom; whereas with plants it is still at a loss. Humanity will work over and transform the whole mineral kingdom. To a large extent this will happen through oscillating electricity that no longer needs wires. (GA 93a, 29 September 1905)

Once humanity has absorbed the whole mineral kingdom in this way during the present physical Stage of Form, the fruits of this work will then be further elaborated in the following Stage of Form, and completely spiritualized by the last Stage of Form of this Round, the arupa condition. They are then carried over into the subsequent Life Stage.

When, at the end of the present physical Stage of Form, the earth takes on supersensory form once more, it will first pass over:

into an etheric earth, then an astral earth. . . . On the previous astral earth Jehovah and his hosts gave human beings their form. But on the sculptural-astral earth human beings will give themselves their form out of their own inner strength, and this is why it is called the sculptural Globe. The following Globes—the rupa and arupa Globes—behave in a similar way. The human being must refine himself completely until in the end he is only like a seed, a seminal condition of everything he has absorbed. All experiences are concentrated in him at the end as though in a point of energy. The seeds that were present in the first Globe did not yet contain this. But in the final Globe the seeds contain everything they have experienced during the previous Globes. (GA 93a, 26 October 1905)

At the end of the physical Globe we will have everything like a reflection in the Ego. When we have everything inside us, we will shape everything from within outwards. This is the 'sculptural' aspect of the next Globe. The architect of Cologne Cathedral combined everything in his inner being; and this content of his Ego becomes enlivened by buddhi, and during the fifth Globe he will shape everything *sculpturally*. In the sixth Globe this will all exist as thoughts, and in the seventh it will all be drawn back into the atom. In the next Round humanity will create a new plant kingdom out of the Ego....

At present we are in the middle Globe, the fourth. In the fifth Globe we will develop the ability to organize ourselves from within. The earth will have turned into a sphere in which the human being enlivens his form from within outwards. The earth is then a 'sculptural' Globe. The sixth Globe will be one in which human beings not only sculpt their own shape but are able to incorporate their own thoughts into this shape. In the fifth Globe a human being can shape a hand for himself, for example; in the sixth, he can send out his thoughts. In the seventh Globe everything becomes formless once more. Everything goes back into a seed state. (GA 93a, 28 October 1905)

For this description of the Stages of Form of the fourth Life Stage of the earth, Rudolf Steiner gives the following names:

1. Arupa = tendency towards form
2. Rupa = form
3. Astral = shining, glittering from within
4. Physical = impenetrable in space
5. Sculptural = shaping from within
6. Intellectual
7. Archetypal (GA 93a, 27 October 1905)

And what is gained in experience and understanding during the whole fourth Life Stage in the *mineral kingdom*, is carried over as fruit into the next Life Stage, the plant-kingdom stage. At the beginning of this fifth Life Stage, during its arupic first Stage of Form, the results of the previous four Life Stages, working as energizing impulses in the points of thought-seed, will determine further evolution.

[After a brief pralaya] the earth passes into the new arupic condition of the next, the fifth Round, then into a rupa-mental condition, and then

> into an astral one. It then appears physically again. Everything that man worked into the mineral kingdom during the fourth Round appears again and, during the fifth Round, grows into a plant kingdom; for example, Cologne Cathedral will grow in the next Round as a plant. . . . In the fifth Round the previous mineral kingdom emerges in all its forms as a plant kingdom. The arupic condition of the fifth Round contains everything that humanity had worked on in the mineral Round. This appears initially in the arupic condition, in pure akasha. Hence one calls this condition 'akasha'. (GA 93a, 5 October 1905)

> We are not working in vain when we shape the mineral kingdom today. Machines, Cologne Cathedral, will grow as a plant world out of what will then be the ground. In the atmosphere of the fifth Round we find the paintings of today as living cloud formations. We are dealing with a recapitulation at a higher level, where all our work in the mineral world is growing around us. (GA 93a, 26 October 1905)

What appears as 'sculpturally' formed in the astral during the fifth—the astral—Stage of Form of the fourth Life Stage of the earth, will in the fifth Life Stage grow out of the ground as a plant in physical form. In the fifth Life Stage this will of course occur in the astral; this plant-being will only take shape physically in the fourth stage of the Jupiter period.

After the fifth Life Stage, the stage of the plant kingdom, the earth will pass over to the sixth, the stage of *the animal kingdom.*

> In the sixth Round there will no longer be a plant kingdom. At that time man will release living sentient thoughts into his surroundings in the form of purely intellectual structures. During the sixth Principal Age of the sixth Globe of this sixth Round something significant will be decided. Everything that was able to evolve in all the kingdoms will have arrived at the Devachan condition. If there is anyone who is not advanced enough to be raised to the Devachan level, then he will remain at an animal level. This is decided by the number 666, the number of the beast. (GA 93a, 28 October 1905)

This is followed by the final Life Stage of earth evolution, the stage of *the human kingdom*:

> In the seventh Round humanity has completely purified itself. The 'human kingdom' then gives itself its own engraving. This is the quickest Round; when man emerges from it he is completely spiritualized and makes the evolutionary transition to Jupiter. (GA 93a, 28 October 1905)

> In the fifth Round [the sculptural-astral one], it is no longer necessary for a human being to keep his hands. He forms a hand when he needs one, like a feeler, because everything by that time will have become plant. Every secretion is also a plant product. Thus everything that originates in man is a plant entity. We will then be living in the plant kingdom.
>
> In the sixth Round we will be living in the animal kingdom. Then everything that originates in man, that flows out of him, is a living product with life and sentience in it. A word becomes a living being, a bird that one sends out into the world.
>
> In the seventh Round man creates himself. He is then capable of constantly doubling, of multiplying himself.... Then our Ego is the bearer of all earth experiences. (GA 93a, 27 October 1905)

> In the fifth Round we redeem the plant world; in the sixth, the animals; and in the seventh, the human kingdom. Then the human being is sufficiently mature to progress to a new planet. (GA 93a, 26 October 1905)

The fourth Life Stage of the earth—the mineral kingdom—is the only one in which development descends to the sense-perceptible level, and this only during the course of the present, fourth Stage of Form—the physical stage. All future evolutionary stages will take place in the supersensory worlds once more. Thus, in the fifth Life Stage of the earth—the plant kingdom—evolution will descend only as far as the astral plane; in the sixth Life Stage—the animal kingdom—to the rupa plane; and in the seventh Life Stage—the human kingdom—the entire passage through the Stages of Form will unfold within the arupa condition, as was the case in the first Life Stage of the earth.

What man will have worked on in the fifth Life Stage of earth evolution on the astral plane in the plant kingdom, he will structure and shape down at the physical level on Jupiter. What he will have worked on in the sixth Life Stage on the rupa plane in the animal kingdom, he will structure and shape at the physical level during Venus. And what he will have worked on in the seventh Life Stage of earth in the human kingdom, he will structure and shape at the physical level on Vulcan. Just as, by the end of the earth period, man will be fully embodied in the mineral kingdom, so he will be embodied in the plant kingdom on Jupiter, in the animal kingdom on Venus, and in the human kingdom on Vulcan. The human being will then be perfected and able to rise to a higher existence. Thus the potentials implanted into man by higher powers are elaborated cycle by cycle to ever higher levels, and to the highest perfection.

II. THE ELEMENTAL WORLD

1. The elemental world as the world of etheric forces

The elemental world is the same as the astral or soul world. It is the aspect of the astral world that activates all the formations of physical, etheric and astral existence, thus also the structure of the members-of-being of earthly creatures. 'When the human being lives into the elemental world, he becomes aware that his own bodily nature—meaning here the full bodily nature, including the higher members of human nature—is structured out of this elemental world.' (GA 119, 26 March 1910) The same applies to the members-of-being of minerals, plants, and animals. And the elemental world re-absorbs into itself the bodily sheaths of these creatures when they die. When the human soul has stepped through the portal of death, it lays aside the etheric body and lives on in its astral body. The etheric body dissolves with everything that had been worked into it by the soul during the life just ended. The etheric body:

> is changed in the elemental world; it is absorbed into the beings that comprise the elemental world. . . . The soul experiences the processes in this elemental world after death *as its outer world.* This experiencing of the elemental world *from the outside* is described in {my books} *Theosophy* and *Occult Science* as the passage of the soul through the *soul world.* [During the time the etheric body is undergoing its changes] the human being lives in the astral body and, from the perspective of clairvoyant consciousness, is in what can be called the elemental world. (GA 147, 31 August 1913)

After death, the soul in the astral world experiences the dissolution of the etheric body into the soul or elemental world. The elemental world shows itself to the perceiving gaze of the seer as the totality of all the etheric forces that structure the physical, etheric, and astral bodies of beings on earth. Hence the elemental world is essentially the same as the etheric world. Thus Rudolf Steiner speaks of the life-body of the earth as its 'elemental body' (GA 17, 'The human etheric body and the elemental world'), and also of the human being experiencing himself in his 'elemental or etheric body'. (GA 138, 26 August 1912)

It can certainly be difficult to find one's way through the plethora of elemental or etheric beings since their names are not unambiguous. Rudolf Steiner usually mentions etheric beings or elemental beings without defining more closely which kind he means. In the physical world things appear with solid contours and can therefore be named unambiguously. In the elemental world everything interpenetrates and changes its form. Very often beings merge into one another; they can appear to the seer from different aspects for which modern language has as yet no adequate expression. Thus different phenomena have to be described with the same words, or the same phenomena with different words, depending on the standpoint from which they are regarded. 'When a spiritual scientist wishes to describe the higher worlds, he must use words taken from language that is adapted for ordinary life. He can only speak in similes; he can try to choose his words so that gradually an idea or picture is awakened of what is perceived through spiritual perception.' (GA 119, 26 March 1910) Thus it can only be a matter of trying to get an approximate overview of the beings of the elemental world, without being completely definitive.

A clear demarcation between the elemental world and the physical on the one hand, and the astral on the other, is also not possible because the physical and astral worlds partially interpenetrate. Rudolf Steiner describes a boundary between these two worlds as follows.

> When I say ... 'on the border between the physical and the astral plane', don't imagine a {clear-cut} boundary line. If we start with the physical plane, we have here ... seven sub-divisions of the physical; then we get seven sub-divisions of the astral plane. Of these {astral sub-divisions} the three lowest coincide with the three highest sections of the physical plane. We need to regard the astral and physical planes as coinciding in so far as the three highest sections of the physical plane are simultaneously the three lowest sections of the astral plane. (GA 101, 27 December 1907)

There can also be ambiguity therefore when statements are made that on one occasion refer to the astral plane and on another to the physical, but without it always being clear which is meant.

We can note in passing here that the astral plane and lower Devachan are also interwoven in the same way as the physical and astral planes. Thus Rudolf Steiner talks on one occasion of 'that part of the astral world that is to be counted along with the lower Devachan'. (GA 130, 18 November 1911) Upper and lower Devachan are presumably likewise interconnected. This also helps us understand statements by the spiritual researcher about the appearance of Christ Jesus in the supersensible. In our present fifth post-Atlantean cultural epoch a reappearance of Christ Jesus is beginning 'in etheric form on the astral plane'; in the sixth cultural epoch he will manifest 'in astral form in the lower Devachan world', and in the seventh cultural epoch as spirit-form, 'in the form of the greatest 'I', as the spiritualized Ego-Self in upper Devachan'. (GA 130, 4 November 1911)

Elemental beings are etheric beings. *Ether* is a supersensory, non-spatial force that is a direct polarity to the physical.

> If we picture to ourselves that earthly forces spread out from the earth on all sides, and the human being lives within these forces which are those of the physical world, then we must imagine the etheric world coming towards the physical forces from all sides, from the whole sphere of the cosmos, and thus approaching man. (GA 84, 22 April 1923)

The physical works in the earth as gravity, pushing down, contracting to a central point, solidifying, rigidifying; the etheric works expansively as levity, spreading out, dissolving. The physical forces of gravity are central forces; the etheric forces of levity are universal or light forces. Central forces operate from a central point; universal forces work in from the cosmic periphery which we can think of as being represented by the sun. The physical condenses matter to a solid state; ether loosens matter and releases it more or less from earthly laws and weight. The physical fills space with matter; the etheric not only empties space by, as it were, sucking matter into itself, dissolving it and making it vanish, but even destroys space itself, creates a gap so to speak, negative space that is not only empty but more than empty. Physical and etheric, gravity and levity, operate together in all earthly things, maintaining more or less of a balance between each other.

As bearer and mediator of life forces, ether activates all growth, germination and sprouting. It is 'the world of coming-into-being and passing-away; and what lies behind it is reigning wisdom ... that truly exists, and whose effects are actually expressed here. And wherever it {wisdom} withdraws so to speak from reality, death arises; wherever it enters, growth arises, and there is coming-into-being, germinating, sprouting life.' (GA 134, 28 December 1911) The human being dives with his physical and etheric body into this etheric world during sleep and draws new enlivening forces from it. 'When we go to sleep, a relationship is established between the physical and etheric body with the whole cosmos, ... our physical and etheric bodies really live in what we call the elemental world.' (GA 159, 7 May 1915)

All together there are seven etheric archetypal or formative forces 'that operate in the cosmos, of which only four, however, reveal themselves in the temporal-spatial processes of our present phenomenal world'. (Guenther Wachsmuth: *Die ätherischen Bildekräfte in Kosmos, Erde und Mensch*, Chap 2)* These are: warmth-ether, light-ether, tone-ether, and life-ether. Tone-ether is also called sound-, number-, form-, and chemical-ether. The warmth and light states of matter can be perceived directly by man. Tone-ether, on the other hand, is:

> something that initially does not manifest at all for us in its original form; what we can perceive in the physical world as tone or sound is only a reflection, a sort of shadow of this ether. Behind external sound there is something of a very subtle etheric nature, something spiritual, so that we must describe physical tone only as a shadow of spiritual tone, of the tone- or number-ether. The fourth ether region is life-ether, that which is behind all actual life. . . .
>
> Everything at the soul level is assigned, so to speak, to certain etheric substances. What we call *will* is expressed etherically in what we call *fire*. . . . What we call *feeling* is expressed in the part of the etheric body corresponding to light-ether. Because this is the case, the clairvoyant sees human will impulses like flames of fire that shoot through the etheric body and radiate into the astral body; and he sees feelings as light forms. However, what we experience in our soul as thinking, and which we express in words, is also only a shadow of thinking. . . . Words have their organ in tone-ether; words are forms of expression for thoughts. These forms of expression fill etheric space by sending their vibrations through the tone-ether. And tone is in fact only the shadowy reflection of the actual vibrations of thoughts. But that which is the inner nature of all our thoughts, which gives them meaning, belongs in its etheric condition to the actual life-ether. . . .
>
> After the luciferic influence during the Lemurian period, of these four forms of ether only the two lower ones, fire-ether and light-ether, remained at man's disposal for his free use. The two higher ethers on the other hand, were withdrawn from man. This is the inner meaning when we hear that after man had attained to discerning good and

* Oskar Kürten, following Guenther Wachsmuth, is making a common mistake here of equating etheric forces with formative ones. They are in fact two completely separate sets of forces. However, formative forces, which are zodiacal and planetary forces, do work *through* the ethers, which has led to the confusion. Although there are four or seven ethers (depending on the aspect under consideration), there are a great many more formative forces. For further clarification see *The Etheric* by Ernst Marti.

> evil—expressed pictorially as eating of the Tree of Knowledge—he was prevented from eating of the Tree of Life. This means that what would have permeated thought-ether and meaning-ether freely and arbitrarily, was withdrawn from him. . . . Every human being was given arbitrary power where his will is concerned; he can assert his will as something 'personal'. The same applies to his feelings. . . . But the individual element immediately ceases when we rise from feelings to thinking—indeed even already to the expression of thoughts, to words on the physical plane. While every person's will and feelings are something personal, we come immediately into a common element when we shift into the world of words and thoughts. {Mathematical thought, for example, is not a matter of individual taste or opinion, nor are the words we share in a common language.} . . . Thus everywhere on earth we find individual people with individual feelings and individual will impulses; but we have everywhere the same thinking, the same language among the nations. (GA 114, 21 September 1909)

Elemental etheric forces are behind all the phenomena of the sense-perceptible world, including the physical conditions of matter: warmth-ether behind physical warmth, light-ether behind air, sound-ether behind the watery element, and life-ether behind the solid. Elemental light is the element 'that out of spirit-depths, weaving fruitfully in space, reveals the creating of the gods', the element of which light, which makes all sense-phenomena perceptible, is only an external expression. This elemental light is also the life element of all earthly creatures. 'Light from the sun is not only light but the power for life, for torrential life.' (GA 56, 26 March 1908) In elemental tone- or sound-ether are the forces 'which organize chemical processes, that direct the inter-calibration of substances, . . . that differentiate substance, separate and combine.' Sound-ether, which is a reflection of the harmony of the spheres, orders material existence according to number and measure, and brings about chemical bonds and splits. This ether 'which has a tone- or sound-like nature, of which the sense-perceptible sound that the sensory ear hears is only the external expression, an expression that has passed through the air', permeates the elemental light-ether. And sound-ether 'which differentiates space, permeates it and orders matter', is in turn permeated by what can be called the 'most subtle etheric condition', the life-ether. Life-ether 'permeates, infiltrates sound-ether so that the sound our mouth utters is permeated in us by the meaning of the thought, by that which changes sound into word. What weaves in sound-ether as a finer etheric element, what weaves cosmically through it and gives meaning to the ordering cosmic sound [is] the Word that weaves through space, that pours itself into the sound-ether, and is at the same time the source of life; it is real weaving, swelling life.' (GA 122, 18 August 1910)

As etheric beings, we may assume that all elemental beings are detachments or offspring of the Thrones and the beings of the second hierarchy, for it was these beings who, by offering up the substance of their own being, introduced etheric forces into evolution: warmth-ether from the Thrones during Saturn; light-ether from the Spirits of Wisdom during Sun; tone-ether from the Spirits of Movement during Moon; and life-ether from the Spirits of Form during the earth period (see Chapter 5). This release of etheric forces by higher powers must be understood as the separating-off of non-independent beings with corresponding forces. Even though the management of etheric forces in the course of evolution was passed on from the original powers to other spirit powers—like, for example, the management of warmth-ether from the Thrones to the Spirits of Form (see Chapter 7.2)—the etheric beings would have remained the same, just as the group souls of the kingdoms of nature remained the offspring of the same higher beings from which they originated, even though the kingdom of beings which they served as group souls changed (see Chapter 6.2).

The elemental kingdom divides into three principal groups of etheric beings who shape earthly existence using the formative thought-forces of the elementary kingdoms:

1. *Physical-elemental beings*: elemental beings of the lower divisions of the physical plane who shape the lifeless mineral level using the forces of the first elementary kingdom.
2. *Etheric-elemental beings*: ethers of the higher divisions of the physical plane who shape the living vegetative level using the forces of the second elementary kingdom.
3. *Astral-elemental beings*: ethers of the astral plane who shape the sentient animal level using the forces of the third elementary kingdom.

Thus we can also regard the *elemental world* in its three aspects as *the totality of etheric beings that bring to manifestation in physical, etheric, and astral forms the formative forces of cosmic thought of the three elementary kingdoms.*

Elemental beings, the three principal groups of which divide in turn into numerous super- and sub-groups, do not work alone but with and in one another. Thus, for example, only the solid element is governed exclusively by the physical forces of the first elementary kingdom. In the fluid element the forces of the first elementary kingdom are joined by those of the second. In the airy element the astral forces of the third elementary kingdom are also at work; and in the warmth element, the forces of the fourth kingdom. 'When we penetrate initially into the watery element we experience the world as a great living thing, for we are immediately led out into the cosmos with its wellsprings of life. We experience the world as a living thing. When we come into the rhythmic element [the air element] we experience the world as something permeated with soul; and when we penetrate into the warmth element we experience the world as something permeated by spirit.' (GA 205, 28 June 1921)

Thus in the human physical body, which is composed of a solid, a liquid, an airy, and a warmth organism, only the solid organism is governed exclusively by the physical forces of life-ether. In our fluid organism, the basis of our life of mental picturing, the etheric body is working through the chemical-ether. Our airy organism, the bearer of our feelings, is activated by the astral body through light-ether. And in our warmth organism the Ego stimulates its will impulses through the warmth-ether. (GA 202, 12 December 1920, not quoted)

Hence the human being has a relationship to the gnomes through his physical body, to the undines through his etheric body, to the sylphs through his astral body, and to the salamanders through his Ego. In another way, gnomes, undines, and sylphs, according to their natures, are related to human thinking, feeling, and willing. 'The elemental beings of the solid element are related, inwardly related, to human intellect; the elemental beings of the fluid element are related to human feeling; the elemental beings of the airy element are related to human will. (GA 211, 11 June 1922) Because of this relationship of the elemental beings with the human soul forces, it is possible for other beings—both good and bad—to exert an influence through the elemental beings into the thinking, feeling, and willing of human beings.

2. Attributes of the elemental world

The elemental world is the foundation of the physical one. 'Only when the clairvoyant gaze has penetrated what is given in the seventy or so external elements of science, and looks for the basis of these solid elements, for the forces that bring matter into a solid state—only once one has penetrated behind sensory existence does one find the forces that construct, fashion, compose what is solid, fluid and aeriform in the occult sense.' (GA 122, 20 August 1910)

The *physical world*, like all worlds that serve evolution, is composed of seven divisions. 'In nature we distinguish

solid
fluid
aeriform
warmth-ether
light-ether
chemical-ether and
life-ether.

These are the seven levels of matter.' (GA 93a, 4 October 1905)

Since warmth can express itself both physically and etherically, we get four lower and four upper divisions of the physical plane. The lower divisions comprise the physical and mineral states of matter that present themselves to sense-perception. The beings operating within these divisions are etheric formative forces working as forces of nature with physical laws. Spiritual science calls them *elemental beings*, and distinguishes them according to the four kinds of ether in four principal groups: gnomes (earth beings), undines (water beings), sylphs (air beings), and salamanders (fire beings).

To the upper divisions belong the etheric beings proper who work with etheric laws in earth existence. 'The etheric begins with the first etheric condition which we call the fire-ether condition, or simply fire.' (GA 114, 21 September 1909)

However, in occultism these etheric beings are classed as belonging to the physical plane. Hence on occasion Rudolf Steiner gives a different enumeration of the seven divisions of the physical. 'Let us stay with the four lower divisions of the physical plane, leaving aside the etheric world.' (GA 93a, 30 October 1905) With life-ether we are 'dealing with the most rarefied ether, with the most rarefied physical condition of all.' (GA 11,

'The Life of the Earth') The etheric bodies of plants, animals, and man are composed of warmth-, light-, tone-, and life-ether. Therefore the substance of etheric bodies also belongs to the material of the physical plane. 'What goes over and beyond this [nerve matter] is the beginning of the supersensory levels. It is here that the human etheric body comes into consideration because it is supersensory, consisting today of the very finest material, of that which appears like the most rarefied spray of etheric mist, and which is the foundation of matter that is even finer than nerve matter.' (GA 134, 30 December 1911)

The *elemental world* also has seven divisions.

> Let us look at the elemental level which, being the next level we can reach, lies behind our physical existence, behind what our senses can perceive. Let us look at the elemental existence which is characterized in spiritual science as lying behind the elements of
>
> the earthy
> the watery
> the airy
> the fiery or warmth-related
> the light-related
> the sound-etheric
> the life-etheric. (GA 122, 22 August 1910)
>
> Thus we can describe the elemental existence of the earth as follows. Again we have warmth as the middle condition. As condensed states {from warmth} we have aeriform, fluid, and solid; but as rarefied conditions we have light-, sound-, and life-ether. (GA 122, 20 August 1910)

Thus in the elemental world we need to distinguish an upper and a lower region, connected to one another by warmth; warmth belongs to both regions. The use of the same terminology for the divisions of both the physical and the elemental levels can of course easily lead to misunderstanding by thinking of the physical when, in a spiritual-scientific sense, it is the elemental level that is being discussed. The physical and elemental are two completely distinct worlds despite interweaving and interpenetrating one another.

The elemental world reveals itself to supersensory sight as a strange region of existence difficult to understand. It shows itself to the seer as a world of sense qualities without a substance that has these qualities, as a world of free-floating qualities without things to which they are attached.

> One is dealing there with the qualities of things but not with things. From dense, heavy, physical bodies, only the denseness remains, but not the substance; from fluid bodies only the 'fluidity' remains, but not the substance, not the water or fluid. From air only the 'wanting-to-expand-in-all-directions' remains, but not the substance. One grows into the qualities of objects but one has the feeling one is growing only into the qualities, that the actual objects vanish from one, that all materiality ceases. (GA 144, 3 February 1913)

> [And on another occasion we find:] We perceive something there that we can't get into, so to speak . . . that we could describe by saying that something is before me, be it a being or a thing of the elemental world, and I can only regard it by walking around it; it has an interior and an exterior. Beings of this kind in the elemental world are called 'earth'. Then there are also things and beings in the elemental world which we could describe by using the word we use for what is fluid in the sense world. We can say that the impressions in the elemental world are such that we can see through them to a certain extent, can penetrate into their interior; that, through certain senses that we will speak about later, we have the feeling that, just as we can put our hand into fluid water, so we can also dip into the interior of these things and beings. . . . In the elemental world, we call this 'water'. When earth and water are mentioned in spiritual-scientific books, they are meant in the sense I have just described for you. . . . Physical water is just an external simile for what one sees when one has reached this stage of development. Water is something that pours through the elemental world so to speak, and which you can put your hand into—not in a physical sense, of course, but for the senses of the initiate, for the capacity of spiritual perception. (GA 119, 26 March 1910)

The situation is similar for elemental air and elemental fire in relation to the physical phenomena of air and fire. 'If you make a kind of comparison in your mind between external fire that can burn your finger, and this fire [soul fire], and take what is in the middle between these two, you will get an idea of what is called elemental fire.' (GA 119, 26 March 1910)

Living warmth comes to expression in human beings and higher animals in warm-bloodedness. Warmth also acts as living warmth in plants and the lower animals. Externally perceptible warmth appears in minerals; it is a dead warmth. Inner soul warmth is particularly stimulated in human beings by enthusiasm for ideals and by compassion for other beings.

As soon as one lives into the elemental world.... Initially one grows together with the things and beings and facts of the spiritual world.... It is now the case that, when we really become aware of the element of fire in the elemental world, we feel the fiery element as merged with us, so to speak. We feel ourselves to be inside the object. This feeling of being inside the object can also occur, however, with the other elements. Only the earth element, in a certain sense, is an exception here ... [I]n the elemental world we call anything 'earth' that actually repels us, that one does not want to approach in the elemental world. (GA 119, 28 March 1910)

Thus, in the supersensory world immediately bordering the physical world, there is a state of existence that is impenetrable like solid physical things. A watery and airy state can likewise be experienced there, as in the sense world. While describing Essene initiation, Rudolf Steiner also speaks of astral—that is, elemental—beings that 'appear impenetrable' because they 'want to reveal themselves outwardly', and in ancient Hebrew were called *Nezach*. Impenetrability is a characteristic attribute of the physical; it is 'an asserting of oneself in space that leads to the excluding of others, ... so that two bodies cannot occupy the same place'. (GA 123, 8 September 1910) The free-floating qualities of the elemental world are *elemental states with physical laws*; they are the substance forces of the lower divisions of the elemental level.

When we look around us during the day, all things, no matter what they are, show themselves to us in the following states: the solid state, fluid state, aeriform or gaseous state, and as {degrees of} warmth. As you know, these are always the attributes of an external body, for an external body can be solid like ice, can also be fluid as when ice melts, and can be aeriform as when the melted ice vaporizes. Each of these three states is permeated by what we call warmth {or temperature}. Fundamentally, this is how it is with every thing and being in the external sense-perceptible world.

Now things in the elemental world are such that there are no objects there in the way we come across them in the sense world; in their place we have in the elemental world what in the sensory world are just qualities or attributes.... When we are talking about elemental fire, you need to be aware again that what we know as fire in the physical world is only a simile of it, ... We can really only describe the other three states of the elemental world by saying that water, air, and earth are similes of these three states. (GA 119, 26 March 1910)

In the elemental world one state cannot change into another. But even in the physical world the states change from one to the other only for the external view, as when ice changes into water, and water into vapour. The etheric beings who bring about the various states also act here as individual forces that take over from one another when a state changes. 'As long as etheric formative forces are connected to the bodies of the phenomenal world, they maintain the state they induce only until free etheric forces of a different kind, or stronger ones of the same kind, bring about a change in the state' (Guenther Wachsmuth, *Die ätherischen Bildekräfte in Kosmos, Erde und Mensch*, Chapter 2).

3. The structuring of the ethers in the earth's physical Stage of Form

During the previous embodiments of the earth, on Saturn, Sun, and Moon, evolution at each physical Stage of Form took place at the elemental level of existence. This still applied to the earliest periods of physical earth evolution. For example, what is portrayed in Genesis as the six days of creation, took place in the elemental sphere. It presents the creation of the physical world in an elemental state of existence that would only be perceptible to the clairvoyant eye. Only during the Lemurian period, when minerality was introduced into earth existence, did the present physical and material states of matter condense out of the elemental state. (GA 122, 20 August 1910, not quoted)

After the phase of rest (pralaya) between the astral and physical conditions of form of present earth evolution, the ethers that existed hitherto re-emerged at an elemental level. 'On earth we thus have seven states of elemental nature, just as on Old Saturn we had only one, a middle one, the warmth condition. Hence we need to imagine our earth—as it rose at the beginning of its present existence out of cosmic darkness, and was still united with the sun and the other planets—as weaving and living in these seven elemental conditions.' (GA 123, 3 September 1910) The earth was then in its first Principal Age, the Polarean period.

At first the seven elemental conditions still rested in the highest and most subtle type of ether that evolution had hitherto produced—elemental life-ether. In his book *The Akashic Chronicle*, Rudolf Steiner describes how the other types of ether emerged from this subtlest life-ether during the physical Stage of Form. A soul seed remained behind from the earth's astral Stage of Form, in which rested the forces from which the new physical condition of form was to arise. At the beginning of this physical condition of form, the earth consisted only of elemental life-ether. The earth appears to the seer at this point as 'a sphere composed in turn of innumerable small etheric spheres'. Elsewhere, Rudolf Steiner describes this primal earth '. . . like a mist, like a rarefied etheric cloud . . . as though composed of myriads of subtle etheric points'. (GA 106, 3 September 1908)

Out of this single 'life-ether-substance' two others separate out to begin with, the denser one of the two being similar to our present air, while the more rarefied one brought it about 'that chemical elements form out of the previously undivided substance.... Here we will call this type of ether "chemical ether".... There remained alongside this a residue of the earlier substance, of the life-ether. Only a portion of the life-ether separates into the two conditions mentioned. We are now dealing in the physical earth with three kinds of substance.' What had arisen as the finer substance consisted of elemental chemical ether, whereas the aeriform substance was elemental air. Both new substances split once more: 'The aeriform substance divided into two, the denser of which becomes watery, the other remains aeriform. But the chemical ether also divides into two separate substance conditions; one becomes denser and forms what we will call light-ether.... But a portion of the chemical ether remains as it was.' This took place during the second Principal Age of the earth, the Hyperborean age.

> We are now dealing with a physical earth that consists of the following conditions of matter: water, air, light-ether, chemical ether, and life-ether.... Now an important cosmic event takes place: the sun separates out {from the earth}. With this, certain forces simply depart from the earth. These forces are composed of a portion of what hitherto had existed on the earth in the life-ether, chemical ether, and light-ether. These forces were now withdrawn, as it were, from what the earth had become up to this point. For the earth, the withdrawal of the sun resulted in a further condensing of matter. Solid matter now begins to form out of the watery condition. Likewise the light-ether divides into another type of light-ether and into an ether that enables bodies to produce warmth. Because of this the earth becomes an entity that can generate heat. All its beings come under the influence of warmth.... Here our look at the Akasha Chronicle has brought us almost to the point of the cosmic catastrophe that was caused by the moon separating off from the earth. (GA 11, 'Beginning of the present Earth')

This last ether to arise from the light-ether is the elemental warmth-ether.

The withdrawal of the sun occurred during the Hyperborean age, and that of the moon during the Lemurian age. At each stage a portion separated out, by a process of condensation, from the most recent substance, whereby the remaining portion was now freed of the lower elements and thus rose higher. 'We are dealing here therefore with a process whereby something higher develops at the cost of something else which it expels from itself.' (GA 11)

This gives us the following sequence in the appearance of the elemental ethers during the present physical Stage of Form:

Life-ether	
Chemical ether	Air
Light-ether	Water
Warmth-ether	Solid

Two groups of elemental states arose separately at different levels. The ethers in the sequence on the left are pure etheric forces of the higher divisions of the elemental level, a portion of which, including the life-ether, withdrew from the earth with the sun, whereas the other portion remained behind. The ethers on the right are the elemental substance-forces of the lower elemental divisions; they are substances in an elemental state of existence without minerality. Even the solid condition, which was the last to form, is still to be thought of in elemental form and therefore not outwardly perceptible. With reference to the hardening of elemental substance, Rudolf Steiner says: 'When we speak about the bodies hardening [before the withdrawal of the moon], we need to understand this not physically but with regard to strength and quality.' (GA 109, 10 June 1909)

The last ether to arise was elemental warmth-ether. 'Warmth is to be thought of as intensive movement in which, in every part of space where warmth exists, there is a striving to generate material existence and to cause material existence to vanish again.' (GA 321, 11 March 1920) Warmth is both etheric and substantial at the same time. Therefore elemental warmth arose together with elemental warmth-ether. At this point all the elemental forces that had arisen in earlier times had emerged again.

There now followed the transition from the elemental to the physical state. With the forces that were intended to work at the mineral level, something new came into evolution. 'A process had to take place at the astral level once more, similar to what had taken place previously: certain beings raised themselves higher at the cost of other beings. A portion of beings separated off who were suited to working on tough, solid matter. And at this point the solid skeleton of the mineral kingdom arose for the earth.' (GA 11, 'The Beginning of the Present Earth') Rudolf Steiner did not indicate how physical forces arose from the elemental ones. If we assume that evolution continued in the way it had hitherto, we can imagine that the 'portion of beings who were suited to working on tough, solid matter' split off from the most recent elemental warmth-ether, and that a division occurred within this separated portion whereby 'certain beings raised themselves higher at the cost of other beings'. This means that a portion of the separated elemental warmth-ether condensed to physical substance-forces of warmth with the tendency 'to generate material existence' by connecting with the mineral level. Through this the other part of the separated elemental warmth-ether was purified of lower constituents, rose higher, and became physical warmth-ether with the tendency 'to cause material existence to vanish'.

A portion of these physical warmth-substance forces then condensed to physical substance-forces of air, a process which, according to a general cosmic law, was connected with the simultaneous creation of light-ether. By further processes of condensation and refinement there arose the substance-forces of physical water and physical solids, as well as physical chemical ether and physical life-ether. Thus to the seven previous elemental divisions were added the seven physical ones, the so-called 'etheric formative forces'.* The beings of the lower divisions of the physical plane are the elemental beings who engage directly with the mineral level and thereby bring about the phenomena of the sense world.

The unfolding of the ethers had begun at the physical Stage of Form with the 'finest' ether, elemental life-ether, and finished with the emergence of physical life-ether. 'The process whereby the earth passes initially from the most rarefied etheric matter, condenses, and then returns to a condition of fine physical etheric matter again, is called a Globe. The physical Globe therefore evolves out of a condition that is finer than the finest physical ether.' (GA 93a, 26 October 1905)

The mineral level is caught to begin with by the physical warmth that separated out of elemental warmth. This occurred through a process of combustion following the withdrawal of the sun from the earth. 'And because of this process of combustion, which hadn't existed at all before, substances separated out within the earth mass which in occultism are called *ash*.... Think away the mineral mass, {think of} the whole earth with its beings but still without mineral mass, and then through a process of combustion the depositing of mineral substances.' (GA 102, 16 March 1908) It was through this combustion that dead mineral warmth, resulting from the external combustion of mineral matter, arose in earth existence. Elemental warmth is a living warmth, life-warmth. In earlier times people understood under the term *ash* 'the entire sum of the mineral kingdom which had precipitated out of the cosmic process and had become dead because it is a waste product of what is living'. (GA 221, 18 February 1923)

This combustion took place on the border between the elemental and physical conditions of the earth, because in earth existence physical

*See footnote on page 150.

warmth never appears on its own but always as permeating the other physical states. Thus the earth passed from a fiery-gaseous to a fiery-fluid condition. 'During the Lemurian period, fluid-fiery metal masses arise through the precipitation, so to speak, of fine masses of ash—the first deposits of mineral matter.' (GA 109, 10 June 1909. See also Iwer Thor Lorenzen's *Grundprobleme der Evolution* (Fundamental problems of evolution), Volume I, '*Aus der Frühzeit der Erdenentwicklung* ('Early phases of evolution')', Hamburg 1958). 'Through the subsequent condensing of fluids to solids, the skeleton of the mineral kingdom could finally arise.'

III. THE SPIRITUAL ORGANISM OF THE EARTH—THE PLANETARY SPIRIT

(a fragment)

The substances of the various Stages of Form are structured by immeasurably vast hosts of etheric, elemental, astral, and spiritual beings of a non-independent nature that are detached from higher independent beings. Thus Rudolf Steiner speaks of 'divine powers, working externally, that pour out astral matter and fill the forms with light and colour'. (GA 93a, 28 October 1905) These detached beings are highly diverse in nature depending on the higher powers from which they stem and the tasks they are intended to fulfil in the cosmic plan. Only possessing life and consciousness that is derived from higher beings, they are not independent spiritual entities, but they reveal themselves to the clairvoyant gaze as individual life forms. The lower elemental beings are described as being absorbed again, once they have fulfilled their tasks, into the higher beings from which they originally detached. We may assume the same for the offspring of higher beings. These {offspring} beings are the substance—the Prakriti—out of which spirit beings—the Purusha of minerals, plants, animals, and man—structure their members-of-being. From this perspective what is termed, by way of illustration, 'the condensing of primal substance', involves the living beings of the original neutral cosmic fire connecting themselves at the various Stages of Form with other, increasingly lower, living beings, enveloping themselves in these so to speak, and thus appearing gradually in ever denser forms. And behind these condensing processes stand the effective forces of the elementary kingdoms with their tendencies towards form.

Once we have become accustomed to the idea that everything appearing as substance to our deceiving gaze is the expression of beings and their deeds, then, among other things, a particular statement by the spiritual researcher that sounds so strange, is no longer so incomprehensible: his statement that the matter of a planet becomes more and more compressed towards its centre, and vanishes at its core. And 'everything that vanishes into the core comes back again from the periphery. It is drawn in, but this matter now contains everything that the beings who worked on the planet have elaborated into it, have imprinted into it—not of course in its present form, but in a form they give it through this transformation.' (GA 110, 18 April 1909)

And just as there are living etheric and elemental beings behind what appears as physical substance, and similar beings of an astral nature behind astral substance, so we need to think of the substances that compose the regions of spirit land, which Rudolf Steiner expressly termed living thought-beings, as consisting of non-independent beings of a spiritual nature which have detached from divine-spiritual beings. And we must assume the same with regard to the original neutral cosmic fire, which, by sacrificing substance of their own being, was transformed by the Thrones into thought-seed substance of the physical level. We can imagine this taking place by the Thrones uniting the living beings that formed their spiritualized physical body with the living beings of the neutral cosmic fire. The Thrones thereby freed themselves from Prakriti in order to enter as free souls into pure Purusha.

Thus we see the earth as a living spirit organism composed of an incalculable multiplicity of non-independent supersensory beings of the most diverse kinds. Lower and higher etheric and elemental beings, Spirits of the Cycles of Time, and beings of the Planetary Spirit shape the existence of the earth in their collaboration as servers of higher divine-spiritual beings and as mediators of the forces of the sun and the starry worlds.

Finally, also belonging to the earth—as its Ego, as it were—is the *Planetary Spirit*, which likewise 'consists of many, many units, of wonderful individual spiritual beings'. For as long as the human being, through esoteric training, experiences himself only in his astral body, he still feels connected to everything 'that can only live externally on any territory of our planet'. For this is still connected with the working of the Spirits of the Cycles of Time. But when the human being awakens in his Ego, he feels himself 'immersed in the Planetary Spirit as though in the sea that washes around the whole earth-planet and is the Spirit of the Earth itself.... This Spirit of the Earth has the task of bringing the earth into mutual relationship with the other heavenly bodies around it, to direct and guide it so that in the course of the ages it is correctly positioned in relation to the other heavenly bodies. This Spirit of the Earth is like a great sensory apparatus of the earth, through which the earth planet comes into correct relationship with its surroundings.' (GA 136, 4 April 1912)

And just as the effects of the elemental beings and the Spirits of the Cycles of Time come to expression in the sensory world, so in a certain sense does the Planetary Spirit also.

> If we ask about the meaning of the phenomena of nature, and want to analyse this meaning and construct it from external factors—as deeper philosophy still sometimes tries to do—then we come close to the expression of the Planetary Spirit itself in the physical world. . . . If we look for meaning in the laws of nature, we will be able to perceive this meaning as the expression of the Planetary Spirit in the sensory world. In perceiving meaning in nature, the human being feels himself at least connected with the Spirit of the whole planet, who guides the planet through cosmic space. (GA 136, 4 April 1912)

Nothing is said about the nature or origin of the beings forming the Planetary Spirit. However, from the context in which they are spoken about in connection with nature spirits and the Spirits of the Cycles of Time, we may conclude that we are also dealing here with non-independent offspring of higher divine-spiritual powers. In another place the Cherubim are described as the beings who co-ordinate the individual planets of our {solar} system, whereas it is the Seraphim who regulate the relation of our system with the neighbouring planetary systems around it. (GA 136, 7 April 1912, not quoted) Hence we can assume a connection of the being of the Planetary Spirit with the Cherubim and Seraphim.

Ever since, through the Mystery of Golgotha, Christ united himself with the spiritual portion of the earth, he has been 'the Lord of heavenly forces on earth' (credo of the Christian Community), and thus the leader not only of the planetary spirits but also of all other supersensory beings working in earth existence. Christ is the Planetary Spirit of the Earth who gives it its meaning.

APPENDIX

Overview of Stages of Evolution

Stages of:

	Consciousness (Planetary embodiments)	**Life** (Rounds)	**Form** (Globes)	**Root Races or Principal Ages**	**Post-Atlantean cultural epochs**
1	Old Saturn	1st elementary	Arupa	Polarean	Ancient Indian
2	Old Sun	2nd elementary	Rupa	Hyperborean	Ancient Persian
3	Old Moon	3rd elementary	Astral	Lemurian	Egypto-Chaldean
4	Earth	mineral	Physical	Atlantean	Greco-Roman
5	(future) Jupiter	plant	Astral	Post-Atlantean	Present
6	(future) Venus	animal	Rupa	6th	6th Post-Atlantean
7	(future) Vulcan	man	Arupa	7th	7th Post-Atlantean

Each stage of Consciousness passes through 7 Life Stages or Rounds.
Each Life Stage passes through 7 Stages of Form or Globes.
Each Stage of Form passes through 7 Principal Ages.
Each Principal Age passes through 7 Cultural epochs.

Regions of the Spirit World (Devachan)

Arupa plane (Upper Devachan) **World of Reason** **Intuition**	7	Thought-seeds of the **physical** level	1st Elementary kingdom
	6	Thought-seeds of the **etheric** level	2nd Elementary kingdom
	5	Thought-seeds of the **astral** level	3rd Elementary kingdom
Rupa plane (Lower Devachan) **Mental World** **Inspiration**	4	Mid-point, having a co-ordinating and mediating role. Archetypes of purely human creative **thoughts**	
	3	Archetypes of **astral** forms and astral bodies	
	2	Archetypes of **etheric** forms and etheric bodies	
	1	Archetypes of **physical** forms and physical bodies	

Astral World			
Imagination			

Bibliography

by GA number of the Rudolf Steiner-Gesamtausgabe (complete edition)

GA

4 *The Philosophy of Freedom*

9 *Theosophy*

10 *How to Attain Knowldege of the Higher Worlds*

11 *The Akashic Chronicle*

13 *Occult Science—an outline*

14 *Four Mystery Dramas—The Portal of Initiation; The Soul's Probation; The Guardian of the Threshold; The Soul's Awakening*

17 *Die Schwelle der geistigen Welt. Aphoristische Ausführungen (*The Portal of the Spiritual World—aphorisms)

26 *Anthroposophical Leading Thoughts*

27 *Grundlegendes für eine Erweiterung der Heilkunst nach geisteswissenschaftlichen Erkenntnissen. (*Foundation for a broadening of the art of healing according to spiritual scientific understanding) by Dr Rudolf Steiner and Dr Ita Wegman

54 *Die Welträtsel und die Anthroposophie (*World Riddles and Anthroposophy)

56 *Die Erkenntnis der Seele und des Geistes (*Knowledge of the soul and spirit)

66 *Geist und Stoff, Leben und Tod* (Spirit and matter, life and death)

84 *Was wollte das Goetheanum und was soll die Anthroposophie? (*What did the Goetheanum want and what should anthroposophy do?)

93a *Grundelemente der Esoterik (*Foundations of Esotericism*)*

94 *Kosmogonie. Populärer Okkultism. Das Johannes-Evangelium. Die Theosophie an Hand des Johannes-Evangeliums* (Cosmogony. Popular occultism. St John's Gospel. Theosophy in connection with St John's Gospel)

97 *Das christliche Mysterium* (The Christ Mystery)

98 *Natur- und Geistwesen—ihr Wirken in unserer sichtbarer Welt (*Nature and spirit beings—their working in the visible world)

99 *Theosophy of the Rosicrucians*

100 *Menschheitsentwickelung und Christus-Erkenntnis. Theosophie und Rosenkreuzertum. Das Johannes-Evangelium* (Human development and knowledge of Christ. Theosophy and Rosicrucianism. The Gospel of St John)

101 *Mythen und Sagen. Okkulte Zeichen und Symbole.* (Myths and Sagas. Occult signs and symbols)

102 *Das Hereinwirken geistiger Wesenheiten in den Menschen* (The work of spiritual beings in man)

103 *Das Johannes-Evangelium* (The Gospel of St John)

104 *Die Apokalypse des Johannes (*The Apocalypse of St John)

105 *Welt, Erde und Mensch, deren Wesen und Entwickelung sowie ihre Spiegelung in dem Zusammenhang zwischen ägyptischem Mythos und gegenwärtiger Kultur* (Cosmos, Earth and Man—their evolution and their reflection in the connection between Egyptian myth and modern culture)

106 *Ägyptische Mythen und Mysterien* (Egyptian myths and mysteries)

107 *Geisteswissenschaftliche Menschenkunde* (Study of Man)

109 *Das Prinzip der spirituellen Ökonomie im Zusammenhang mit Wiederverkörperungsfragen. Ein Aspekt der geistigen Führung der Menschheit* (The principle of spiritual economy in connection with questions of reincarnation—an aspect of the spiritual guidance of humanity)

110 *Geistige Hierarchien und ihre Widerspiegelung in der physischen Welt* (Spiritual hierarchies and their reflection in the physical world)

112 *Das Johannes-Evangelium im Verhältnis zu den drei anderen Evangelien, besonders zu dem Lukas-Evangelium* (The Gospel of St John in relation to the other three Gospels, and particularly to the Gospel of St Luke)

113 *Der Orient im Lichte des Okzidents. Die Kinder des Luzifer und die Brüder Christi* (The Orient in the light of the Occident. The children of Lucifer and the brothers of Christ)

114 *Das Lukas-Evangelium* (The Gospel of St Luke)

117 *Die tieferen Geheimnisse des Menschheitswerdens im Lichte der Evangelien* (The deeper mysteries of the evolution of humanity in the light of the Gospels)

119 *Makrokosmos und Mikrokosmos. Die große und die kleine Welt. Seelenfragen, Lebensfragen, Geistesfragen* (Macrocosmos and microcosmos—the great and the small world. Questions of soul, life, and spirit)

121 *Die Mission einzelner Volkseelen im Zusammenhang mit der germanisch-nordischen Mythologie* (The mission of the folk-souls in connection with Germanic-Nordic mythology)

122 *Die Geheimnisse der biblischen Schöpfungsgeschichte. Das Sechstagewerk im 1. Buch Moses* (Mysteries of the biblical creation story—the six days of creation in the first book of Moses)

123 *Das Matthäus-Evangelium* (The Gospel of St Matthew)

128 *Eine okkulte Physiologie* (Occult physiology)

129 *Weltenwunder, Seelenprüfungen und Geistesoffenbarungen* (Cosmic wonders, trials of the soul, and revelations of the spirit)

130 *Das esoterische Christentum und die geistige Führung der Menschheit* (Esoteric Christianity and the spiritual guidance of humanity)

131 *Von Jesus zu Christus* (From Jesus to Christ)

132 *Die Evolution vom Gesichtspunkt des Wahrhaftigen* (Evolution from the perspective of truth)

134 *Die Welt der Sinne und die Welt des Geistes* (The world of the senses and the world of spirit)

136 *Die geistigen Wesenheiten in den Himmelskörpern und Naturreichen* (Spiritual beings in the heavenly bodies and in the kingdoms of nature)

138 *Von der Initiation. Von Ewigkeit und Augenblick. Von Geisteslicht und*

Lebensdunkel (Initiation. Eternity and the moment. Spirit light and life darkness)

141 *Das Leben zwischen dem Tode und der neuen Geburt im Verhältnis zu den kosmischen Tatsachen* (Life between death and re-birth in relation to cosmic factors)

142 *Die Bhagavad Gita und die Paulusbriefe* (The Bhagavad Gita and the letters of St Paul)

144 *Die Mysterien des Morgenlandes und des Christentums* (Mysteries of the East and of Christianity)

147 *Die Geheimnisse der Schwelle* (Mysteries of the Threshold)

148 *Aus der Akasha-Forschung. Das Fünfte Evangelium* (From research in the Akasha—the Fifth Gospel

159 *Das Geheimnis des Todes. Wesen und Bedeutung Mittleuropas und die europäischen Volksgeister* (The mystery of death—the nature and significance of Central Europe and the European folk-spirits)

161 *Wege der geistigen Erkenntnis und der Erneuerung künstlerischer Welanschauung* (Paths of spiritual knowlege and the renewal of an artistic world-view)

162 *Kunst- und Lebensfragen im Lichte der Geisteswissenschaft* (Questions of life and art in the light of spiritual science)

165 *Die geistige Vereinigung der Menschheit durch den Christus-Impuls* (The spiritual union of humanity through the Christ impulse)

167 *Gegenwärtiges und Vergangenes im Menschengeiste* (Past and present in the human spirit)

174a *Mitteleuropa zwischen Ost und West* (Central Europe between East and West)

175 *Bausteine zu einer Erkenntnis des Mysteriums von Golgotha. Kosmische und menschliche Metamorphose* (Building-stones for an understanding of the Mystery of Golgotha. Cosmic and human metamorphses)

177 *Die spirituellen Hintergründe der äußeren Welt. Der Sturz der Geister der Finsternis* (The spiritual background of the external world. The fall of the spirits of darkness)

181 *Erdensterben und Weltenleben. Anthroposophishe Lebensgaben. Bewußtseins-Notwendigkeiten für Gegenwart und Zukunft* (Earthly death and cosmic life. Anthroposophical tasks in life. The consciousness needed for the present and the future)

184 *Die Polarität von Dauer und Entwickelung im Menschenleben. Die kosmische Vorgeschichte der Menschheit* (The polarity of duration and evolution in human life. Cosmic pre-history of humanity)

197 *Gegensätze in der Menschheitsentwickelung. West und Ost—Materialismus und Mystik—Wissen und Glaube* (Polarity in the evolution of humanity. West and East—Materialism and mysticism—science and faith)

198 *Heilfaktoren für die sozialen Organismus* (Healing factors for the social organism)

199 *Geisteswissenschaft als Erkenntnis der Grundimpulse sozialer Gestaltung*

(Spiritual science as an understanding of the basic impusles of social structure)

202 *Die Brücke zwischen der Weltgeistigkeit und dem Physischen des Menschen. Die Suche nach der neuen Isis, der göttlichen Sophia* (Bridges between cosmic spirituality and the physical element of man. The search for the new Isis, the divine Sophia)

205 *Menschenwerden, Weltenseele und Weltengeist. Erster Teil: Der Mensch als leiblich-seelische Wesenheit in seinem Verhältnis zur Welt* (Human evolution, world soul and world spirit. Part One: Man as being of body and soul in relation to the cosmos)

208 *Anthroposophie als Kosmosophie. Zweiter Teil: Die Gestaltung des Menschen als Ergebnis kosmischer Wirkungen* (Anthroposophy and Cosmosophy. Part Two: The structure of man as the result of cosmic influences)

211 *Das Sonnenmysterium und das Mysterium von Tod und Auferstehung. Exoterisches und esoterisches Christentum* (The sun mystery and the mystery of death and resurrection. Exoteric and esoteric Christianity)

214 *Das Geheimnis der Trinität. Der Mensch und sein Verhältnis zur Geistwelt im Wandel der Zeiten* (The mystery of the Trinity. Man and his relation to the spirit world in the course of time)

216 *Die Grundimpulse des weltgeschichtlichen Werdens der Menschheit* (The basic impulse behind the evolution of humanity in world history)

220 *Lebendiges Naturerkennen. Intellektueller Sündenfall und spirituelle Sündenerhebung* (Living study of nature. Intellectual fall and spiritual resurrection)

221 *Erdenwissen und Himmelserkenntnis* (Knowledge of earth and understanding of heaven)

222 *Die Impulsierung des weltgeschichtlichen Geschehens durch geistige Mächte* (Impulses of spiritual powers behind events in history)

223 *Der Jahreskreislauf als Atmungsvorgang der Erde und die vier großen Festeszeiten. Die Anthroposophie und das menschliche Gemüt* (The cycle of the year as the breathing process of the earth, and the four great festivals. Anthroposophy and the human heart and mind)

225 *Drei Perspektiven der Anthroposophie. Kulturphänomene, materialistisches Denken und spirituelle Impulse* (Three perspectives of anthroposophy. Cultural phenomena, materialistic thinking and spiritual impulses)

228 *Initiationswissenschaft und Sternenerkenntnis. Der Mensch in Vergangenheit, Gegenwart und Zukunft vom Gesichtspunkt der Bewußtseinsentwickelung* (Initiation science and star-lore. Man in the past, present and future with regard to the evolution of consciousness)

230 *Der Mensch als Zusammenklang des schaffenden, bildenden und gestaltenden Weltenwortes* (Man as symphony of the creative, shaping and formative Cosmic Word)

231 *Der übersinnliche Mensch, anthroposophisch erfaßt* (Supersensory man from the standpoint of anthroposophy)

235 *Esoterische Betrachtungen karmischer Zusammenhänge. Band I* (Karmic Relationships. Volume I)

237 *Esoterische Betrachtungen karmischer Zusammenhänge. Band III: Die karmischen Zusammenhänge der anthroposophischen Bewegung* (Karmic Relationships. Volume III: karmic relationships of the anthroposophical movement)

238 *Esoterische Betrachtungen karmischer Zusammenhänge. Band IV: Das geistige Leben der Gegenwart im Zusammenhang mit der anthroposophischen Bewegung* (Karmic Relationships. Volume IV: The spiritual life of the present in relation to the anthroposophical movement)

239 *Esoterische Betrachtungen karmischer Zusammenhänge. Band V* (Karmic Relationships. Volume V)

243 *Das Initiaten-Bewußtsein. Die wahren und die falschen Wege der geistigen Forschung* (Initiate consciousness. True and false paths of spiritual investigation)

254 *Die okkulte Bewegung im neunzehnten Jahrhundert und ihre Beziehung zur Weltkultur. Bedeutsames aus dem äußeren Geistesleben und die Mitte des neunzehnten Jahrhunderts* (The occult movement in the nineteenth century and its relation to world culture. Things of significance in the external intellectual life of the middle of the nineteenth century)

260 *Die Weihnachtstagung zur Begründung der Allegemeinen Anthroposophischen Gesellschaft 1923/24* (The Christmas conference for the founding of the General Anthroposophical Society 1923/24)

293 *Allgemeine Menschenkunde als Grundlage der Pädagogik. Pädagogischer Grundkurs, Teil I* (Study of man as the basis of pedagogy. Pedagogical course, Part I)

321 *Geisteswissenschaftliche Impulse zur Enwickelung der Physik. Zweiter naturwissenschaftlicher Kurs: Die Wärme auf der Grenze positiver und negativer Materialität* (Spritual scientific impulses for the development of physics. Second science course: warmth at the boundary of positive and negative materiality)

Further Reading

- Ernst Hagemann, *Vom Wesen des Lebendigen* (Lübeck 1963).
- Guenther Wachsmuth, *Die ätherischen Bildekräfte in Kosmos, Erde und Mensch.*
- Iwer Thor Lorenzen, *Grundprobleme der Evolution. Volume 1. Aus der Frühzeit der Erdenentwicklung* (Hamburg 1958)

See also (in English):
Ernst Marti, *The Etheric, Volumes I and II* (Temple Lodge Publishing)

A note from the publisher